Success

International English Skills
for Cambridge IGCSE™

WORKBOOK

Mark Little & Marian Barry

Shaftesbury Road, Cambridge CB2 8EA, United Kingdom

One Liberty Plaza, 20th Floor, New York, NY 10006, USA

477 Williamstown Road, Port Melbourne, VIC 3207, Australia

314–321, 3rd Floor, Plot 3, Splendor Forum, Jasola District Centre, New Delhi – 110025, India

103 Penang Road, #05–06/07, Visioncrest Commercial, Singapore 238467

Cambridge University Press & Assessment is a department of the University of Cambridge.

We share the University's mission to contribute to society through the pursuit of education, learning and research at the highest international levels of excellence.

www.cambridge.org
Information on this title: www.cambridge.org/9781009122665 (Paperback)

© Cambridge University Press & Assessment 2022

This publication is in copyright. Subject to statutory exception and to the provisions of relevant collective licensing agreements, no reproduction of any part may take place without the written permission of Cambridge University Press & Assessment.

First published by Georgian Press (Jersey) Limited 1998
Second edition 2005
Reprinted and published by Cambridge University Press, Cambridge 2010
Third edition 2015
Fourth edition 2017
Fifth edition 2022

20 19 18 17 16 15 14 13 12 11 10 9 8 7 6

Printed in the Netherlands by Wilco BV

A catalogue record for this publication is available from the British Library

ISBN 978-1-009-12266-5 Paperback with Digital Access (2 Years)

Cambridge University Press & Assessment has no responsibility for the persistence or accuracy of URLs for external or third-party internet websites referred to in this publication, and does not guarantee that any content on such websites is, or will remain, accurate or appropriate. Information regarding prices, travel timetables, and other factual information given in this work is correct at the time of first printing but Cambridge University Press & Assessment does not guarantee the accuracy of such information thereafter.

Third-party websites and resources referred to in this publication have not been endorsed by Cambridge Assessment International Education

Cambridge International copyright material in this publication is reproduced under licence and remains the intellectual property of Cambridge Assessment International Education.

....

NOTICE TO TEACHERS IN THE UK
It is illegal to reproduce any part of this work in material form (including photocopying and electronic storage) except under the following circumstances:
(i) where you are abiding by a licence granted to your school or institution by the Copyright Licensing Agency;
(ii) where no such licence exists, or where you wish to exceed the terms of a licence, and you have gained the written permission of Cambridge University Press;
(iii) where you are allowed to reproduce without permission under the provisions of Chapter 3 of the Copyright, Designs and Patents Act 1988, which covers, for example, the reproduction of short passages within certain types of educational anthology and reproduction for the purposes of setting examination questions

DEDICATED TEACHER AWARDS

Teachers play an important part in shaping futures. Our Dedicated Teacher Awards recognise the hard work that teachers put in every day.

Thank you to everyone who nominated this year; we have been inspired and moved by all of your stories. Well done to all of our nominees for your dedication to learning and for inspiring the next generation of thinkers, leaders and innovators.

Congratulations to our incredible winners!

WINNER

Regional Winner Middle East & North Africa	Regional Winner Europe	Regional Winner North & South America	Regional Winner Central & Southern Africa	Regional Winner Australia, New Zealand & South-East Asia	Regional Winner East & South Asia
Annamma Lucy	Anna Murray	Melissa Crosby	Nonhlanhla Masina	Peggy Pesik	Raminder Kaur Mac
GEMS Our Own English High School, Sharjah - Boys' Branch, UAE	British Council, France	Frankfort High School, USA	African School for Excellence, South Africa	Sekolah Buin Batu, Indonesia	Choithram School, India

For more information about our dedicated teachers and their stories, go to
dedicatedteacher.cambridge.org

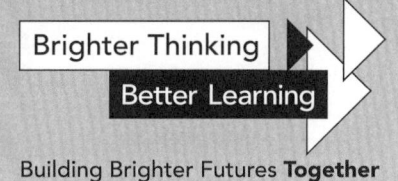

Building Brighter Futures **Together**

› Contents

Introduction	vi
1 Goals and achievements	1
2 Fitness and well-being	18
3 Where we live	33
4 Our impact on the planet	48
5 Entertainment	64
6 Travel and the outdoor life	78
7 Student life	95
8 The search for adventure	110
9 Animals and our world	126
10 The world of work	141
Acknowledgements	157

> Introduction

This Workbook is designed to be used in conjunction with the *Success International English Skills for Cambridge IGCSE™ Coursebook, Fifth edition*. For convenience, many of its exercises are cross-referenced to the Coursebook sections. However, the Workbook can also be used successfully without reference to the Coursebook as the exercises are self-explanatory and complete in themselves. The answers are provided in the *Success International English Skills for Cambridge IGCSE Teacher's Resource, Fifth edition*.

If you are a Cambridge IGCSE English as a Second Language student you will benefit from this book. You will also benefit if you are at upper-intermediate to advanced level and wish to broaden and consolidate your English language ability.

Aims and objectives

The Workbook aims to consolidate and test your understanding of the language and themes introduced in the Coursebook, covering reading, writing and listening skills. For example, the main topic of Unit 1 in the Coursebook is goals, achievements and qualities we admire. The unit focuses on skills for describing people and their qualities, listening to understand speakers' ideas and attitudes, and drafting and redrafting an email. The corresponding Workbook unit follows this up with detailed practice on points of vocabulary related to people and their qualities, a listening task that develops understanding of speakers' opinions and thoughts, and activities to help develop structured emails.

Similarly, Unit 8 teaches story-telling skills, so the corresponding Workbook unit provides a wide variety of exercises to further develop narrative technique.

Flexibility of use

Self-access
You can use the Workbook without help from the teacher, making it suitable for homework and private study.

In the classroom
The Workbook can be used during lessons to complement the work being done with the Coursebook.

Tests
You can use exercises from the Workbook to test your understanding of the material in the Coursebook.

How you will benefit

You are given substantial additional practice in English in activity formats that provide a useful contrast to those in the Coursebook, and which present different kinds of challenges.

Introduction

The Workbook supports achievement by showing you good and not so good examples of language. Text-completion exercises, when finished, provide valuable examples for real-life writing purposes, highlighting the importance of developing writing style, with appropriate tone and register and audience awareness.

The aim of the *Success International* course is to increase your independence by encouraging a mature attitude to learning and an understanding of meaning. The Workbook complements this by encouraging you to work out answers for yourself, to take care in checking your work and to make sure your answers make complete sense.

Range of exercises

The following list is not exhaustive, but gives a flavour of the range of exercises in the Workbook. You are offered plenty of variety to keep you interested and on your toes:

- vocabulary development, idioms, phrasal verbs
- prefixes and suffixes
- listening for gist, detail and implied meaning
- reading for gist, detail and implied meaning
- collocations
- spelling and punctuation
- use of prepositions
- sentence construction
- grammar revision
- textual organisation, logical reasoning and understanding meaning
- paragraphing
- tone and register
- developing writing style
- understanding visual information (maps, graphs and charts).

New to the Fifth edition Workbook:

- pre-listening and listening tasks: there is at least one in each unit
- a minimum of one Grammar spotlight task for each of those presented in the corresponding unit of the Coursebook: all these exercises have been informed by common errors and misconceptions from the Cambridge Learner Corpus.

 The Cambridge Learner Corpus is a multibillion word collection of examples of spoken and written English. We use our corpus to answer questions about English vocabulary, grammar and usage. Along with this, we collect and analyse learner writing. This allows us to clearly see how learners from around the world are similar and different in how they acquire and use language. These insights allow us to provide tailored and comprehensive support to learners at all stages of their learning journey.

Unit 1
Goals and achievements

A Our outlook on life

1 Quick language check

Circle or underline the best word or phrase from each pair in *italics*.

CB Sections A1 to A4

a   George decided to take more responsibility *during / for* his own happiness.
b   Alisha *give / set* herself the goal of starting a business by the time she was 30.
c   Oskar's New Year's *resolution / decision* was to start doing more exercise.
d   If you are really *confident / determined* to achieve something, you'll probably succeed.
e   I think that *eating / eat* more fruit and vegetables is a good idea.
f   What's the best way of *dealing / sorting* with difficult situations?
g   Having a plan for each day helps to give me a real *sense of reason / purpose*.
h   Some people are highly *motivated / encouraged* by the thought of earning lots of money.
i   Lizzie finally told me why *she was / was she* feeling so miserable.
j   It's often incredibly difficult *continuing / maintaining* a work–life balance.

2 Vocabulary check

Use the words in the box to complete the text. You may need to change the form of some of the verbs.

| volunteer   flexibility   pursue   aspirations   honest   obstacles |
| rewards   focus   realistic   admit   process |

Children's **(a)** _____ often change as they get older – one minute they want to be a train driver, the next an astronaut. Khalid, however, knew from a young age that he wanted to become a vet. He realised that it would be a long and difficult **(b)** _____, and that there would be lots of **(c)** _____ to overcome. Despite this, he **(d)** _____ his goal with great determination.

1

Every day at school, he **(e)** _____ on his studies. At weekends, he **(f)** _____ at a local veterinary surgery. He didn't mind working for free, as he knew the experience offered many valuable **(g)** _____ – essential experience with animals, improved chances of being **(h)** _____ to the best university and some excellent contacts in the veterinary field, to name just a few.

Khalid was successful in gaining entry to his preferred university and graduated two years ago. He's now employed by the same surgery he worked at while at school. So what does Khalid say is the key to success? 'I think **(i)** _____ is very important – being able to change your goals if you need to and adapt to any situation are great skills to have. Also, you have to be totally **(j)** _____ with yourself about what it is you really want and whether or not you can actually achieve it. Your goals have to be **(k)** _____, or you'll never achieve them!'

3 Reading for gist

Read this text about Albert Einstein. Circle the correct word from each pair in *italics*.

CB Section A6

A great thinker

How much do you know about Albert Einstein? If you've heard about him but don't know much about his life and work, then read on!

Scientists used to think that matter could not be created nor destroyed. They also believed that the same principles applied to energy. However, in the first few years of the 20th century, the German scientist Albert Einstein came *out / up* with a different idea. He predicted that it should be possible to change mass into energy. Einstein's idea – his Theory of Relativity – was first proved *by / in* 1932. Einstein showed us that a small amount of matter could be changed into a vast amount of energy. This made the development of nuclear energy *available / possible*.

Born in 1879, Einstein was an unusual child; I was fascinated to learn that he didn't speak until he was 3 years old! Early photographs show a serious and intense-looking little boy. When he was 12, he *learnt / taught* himself Euclidean geometry. He hated school, however, and at the age of 15, he used the fact that the family had moved house as an *excuse / explain* for not going to school for a year. He finally graduated in 1900 by studying the lecture notes of a classmate.

Unit 1: Goals and achievements

Einstein grew into a brilliant and *imaginative / imagining* young man who was *passionately / perfectly* interested in science. He was also a very lively correspondent and *did / made* a point of replying to any letters he received from children. His intelligent, friendly face with its untidy mop of silvery hair is well-known, *apart / yet* as a young man he had short, coal-black hair and a serious, thoughtful appearance. The face of the Jedi Master Yoda in the Star Wars films was *copied / inspired* by Einstein's wise expression.

Sadly, Einstein's theories were used to develop nuclear weapons and, ultimately, the atomic bomb. Einstein never *forgave / upset* himself for what his discoveries had led to. Shortly before he died in 1955, he wrote a letter to the newspapers urging scientists to unite to *predict / prevent* the possibility of another nuclear war in the future.

Circle the letter of the correct option to complete these sentences.

1   The text about Albert Einstein is aimed at:

   A   scientists who wish to discover more about his work.

   B   general readers who have an interest in science.

   C   students who want to find out more about careers in science.

2   The purpose of the text is to:

   A   give a detailed description of Einstein's greatest achievements.

   B   suggest reasons why Einstein became such a great scientist.

   C   provide a summary of Einstein's personality, life and work.

4 Style features

Find one example of each of these features.

CB Section A6

a   direct address to the audience

   ....

b   writer making connections with the reader (we/us)

   ....

c   writer sharing information about himself/herself

   ....

d   some informal, conversational language

   ....

5 Figurative language

Replace the figurative language in *italics* with words and expressions from the box.

> CB Section A10

| very sad   very noisy   very proud   disappeared   reminders |
| based on |

a   Irhaa was *bursting with pride* _____ when she talked about the prize she had won.

b   We got a *heart-breaking* _____ letter giving an account of my grandmother's illness.

c   My fear of wasps was *rooted in* _____ the experience of being stung when I was a child.

d   Her anger *melted away* _____ when she saw how sorry the little boy was.

e   There were *echoes* _____ of her own childhood in the novel she wrote about a poor family who emigrated to the USA.

f   There was a *howling* _____ wind all night.

Draw lines to match the figurative expressions to their meanings.

g   move the goalposts   have a single goal you really want to achieve

h   beat yourself up   be able to accept a range of possibilities

i   keep an open mind   achieve far more than those in a similar position

j   set your heart on something   criticise yourself, usually unfairly

k   be a high flyer   achieve a goal you have set yourself

l   reach a milestone   change ambitions, plans or targets

Unit 1: Goals and achievements

Write sentences of your own using each of the figurative expressions g–l.

....

....

....

....

....

....

....

B Facing challenges

1 Comparing information in charts

Study the bar chart showing the connection between literacy and happiness in a European country.

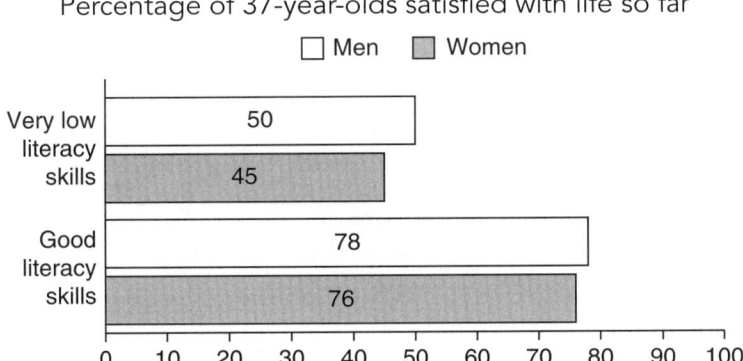

Are statements true or false? Put a tick (✓) if they are true and a cross (✗) if they are false.

a   Less than half the women who had low literacy skills were happy
    with their lives.   _____

b   Men, overall, were more satisfied with their lives than women.   _____

c   More than three-quarters of men and women who had a good
    standard of literacy said they were happy with their lives.   _____

2 Pre-listening task

Complete the definitions using the words and phrases below.

> burst into laughter   roar with laughter   sense of humour
> stony-faced   get into trouble   crack a smile   have a laugh
> laugh along with

a   If you _____, it means you suddenly start laughing.

b   Your _____ is what you do and don't find funny.

c   If you _____, it means your face changes from serious to not serious.

d   If you _____, you laugh in a loud and uncontrolled way, often for a long time.

e   If you _____ with someone, you enjoy your time together in a non-serious way.

f   Someone who is _____ is not showing any emotion and is perhaps in a bad mood.

g   If you _____ someone, you share a joke or a funny moment with them.

h   If you _____, it means you have problems with someone in authority.

3 Listening

You will hear three people talking about what makes them laugh. Match a sentence below with each of the speakers by writing the number of the speaker in the box. There are two extra sentences you do not need to use. Put a cross (X) in the box next to these sentences.

A   I generally laugh at different things to most of my friends.

B   I sometimes laugh when I'm not supposed to.

C   I don't find most comedy films very funny.

D   My best friend is always trying new things to make me laugh.

E   It's actually pretty easy to make me laugh.

Unit 1: Goals and achievements

C Personal qualities

1 Describing character

Match each description of a person's character with a word or phrase from the box. There is one that you do not need.

CB Sections C1 and C2

> sensitive good-natured placid private ambitious optimistic
> artistic untidy absent-minded

a My father tends to forget everyday things and often goes to work without his wallet or laptop.

....

b She gets on well with people and will offer to help you if you need it.

....

c I don't like sitting next to Lian. She leaves apple cores, sweet wrappers and old tissues all over her desk.

....

d Javier is very keen to have a successful career, and he regularly changes his job to improve his prospects.

....

e Their new baby is only two months old, but he hardly cries at all.

....

f The new manager is a very positive thinker and believes in a good future.

....

g Eshe paints lovely pictures and has decorated her home beautifully.

....

h She doesn't share her thoughts and feelings with anyone.

....

2 Vocabulary check

Read the following sentences and decide whether or not they make sense. Tick (✓) the ones that do and put a cross (✗) against the ones that do not. Think carefully about the words in *italics*.

CB Sections C1 and C2

a   My grandfather is such a *bad-tempered* man – he's always in a good mood. _____

b   The radio presenter's *grating* voice was pleasant to listen to. _____

c   *Well-dressed* people have no interest in how they look. _____

d   Gianna has always been *argumentative* – she'd quarrel with herself if she could! _____

e   A *retired* person no longer works for a living. _____

f   Tara took a lot of care over her clothes and make-up, and she always looked *scruffy*. _____

g   The doctor told Wassim he was too *skinny* and should try to put on weight. _____

h   Am I *ambitious*? Definitely. An ordinary life will give me more happiness than making a lot of money or getting a top job. _____

3 Negative prefixes

Make these 16 words into their opposites by writing them after the correct prefix. Use a dictionary if you need to.

CB Section C3

> patient   legal   understand   secure   responsible   literate
> correct   regular   appear   enthusiastic   conscious   significant
> sympathetic   obey   behave   possible

un ....

il ....

im ....

in ....

Unit 1: Goals and achievements

ir...

dis..

mis...

Now choose four of the words you have made and put them in sentences of your own.

....

....

....

....

4 Commenting on positive and negative qualities

CB Section C6

In English, it is common to exaggerate people's positive qualities a little. We also often 'tone down' any negative qualities by using tentative language to avoid criticising someone too much.

Look at the photograph, then read the description of the woman that follows, which was written by her friend. Put the words and expressions in the box into the gaps. Try to exaggerate her positive qualities and tone down any negative ones. Note that some words may fit in more than one gap.

> always incredibly rather absolutely by far can be so
> a little bit great extremely the best slightly

Nadine's my best friend and is **(a)** _____ the nicest person I know. She's a nurse and is **(b)** _____ hard-working. She often works long shifts at the hospital but never complains about it. She's also **(c)** _____ generous, with both her time and her money, and is willing to help **(d)** _____ anyone if she can.

Sometimes, though, Nadine can be **(e)** _____ unreliable if you make an arrangement with her. I've known her to be two hours late, for example, which can be **(f)** _____ annoying. She **(g)** _____ **(h)** _____ difficult to contact too, because she isn't **(i)** _____ at answering her phone!

It's a **(j)** _____ privilege to know Nadine and I'm **(k)** _____ proud to be her friend!

5 Sentence correction

There is an extra word in each of these sentences. Read the sentence carefully and cross out the extra word.

a   I'm really lucky for to know someone as talented as my friend Raphael.
b   Rokia can sometimes seem a little bit of rude, but she's actually just shy.
c   Hassan is one out of the most intelligent people I know.
d   Mathilde is always happy to do that what she can to help others.
e   I don't think I've ever seen Hiroto without a smile on top his face.
f   Kasia and Karolina both them enjoy spending lots of time outdoors.

6 Developing your writing style

This description appeared on a social-media website about family life. Rewrite the description using longer, more complex sentences.

This is my grandmother. She is old. She is small. She has got fair skin. She has got brown eyes. She has white hair. She has a nice personality. She has got a bad leg. She smiles a lot but she has pains in her knee. She has arthritis. She paints pictures of things like birds, animals and flowers. She remembers my birthday. She buys me nice presents. She wears a gold locket around her neck. It is from my grandfather. He bought it for her when they got married. She likes it very much.

Unit 1: Goals and achievements

CB Section C8

SUCCESS INTERNATIONAL ENGLISH SKILLS FOR CAMBRIDGE IGCSE™: WORKBOOK

7 Homophones

**Circle or underline the correct word from each pair in *italics*.
Draw a line through the incorrect word.**

CB Section C11

a   Did you *worn / warn* her about the storm that is forecast for tonight?

b   My grandfather *fought / fort* in the Second World *Wore / War*.

c   Matthew *ate / eight* all the food in the fridge.

d   The curtains I bought in the sale were reduced because there was a *floor / flaw* in the material.

e   Let's go to the beach this weekend, *weather / whether* it rains or not.

f   'Haven't you *groan / grown*!' said Grandma when the children came to visit.

g   We worked really hard on the project and all needed a *break / brake* afterwards.

h   I didn't like the singer's voice, but everyone else thought it was *grate / great*.

Choose four of the words that you crossed out and use each of them in sentences of your own.

....

....

....

....

D People we look up to

1 Sentence correction: Multi-word verbs

CB Section D1

In each of these sentences, a word has been left out of a multi-word verb. Read the sentence carefully, then draw a slash (/) where the missing word goes. Write the word at the end of the sentence.

Example: *She's a strict teacher and doesn't put / with any bad behaviour in her class.* up

a   Olivier really takes his father – they look very similar. _____

b   Chioma's very sociable and gets well with more or less everyone she meets.
    _____

c   Alessandro's really upset because he's fallen with his best friend. _____

d   Pernille treats everyone as though they're equal – she doesn't look down anyone. _____

12

Unit 1: Goals and achievements

e   Ding is someone who will never let you – he's very reliable. _____

f   I look to both of my grandparents as they're both wonderful, kind people. _____

g   Asha and Olga had a massive argument, but made up each other a day later. _____

h   Jimmy is very cheeky, but he gets with it because he's so charming as well. _____

2 Pre-listening task

**Draw lines to match the words to their meanings.
Use a dictionary if necessary.**

a   heritage   not enough of something

b   inhabitant   to encourage someone to do something

c   urge   the government or organisations that have power

d   recover   a difficulty or problem experienced in life

e   authorities   the culture or country that someone comes from

f   shortage   to get better after an illness or accident

g   interpret   a person who lives in a particular place

h   setback   to decide what the meaning of something is

3 Listening

You will hear a student giving a talk about a Mexican artist called Frida Kahlo. Read the sentences and the multiple-choice options, then listen and circle the correct letter for each gap.

CB Section D4

1   Frida's father's family were originally from _____.

   A   South America

   B   Germany

   C   Spain

2   Frida was encouraged to _____ while recovering from an illness called polio.

   A   do sport

   B   try writing

   C   go walking

3 Frida had an accident while _____, which left her in a lot of pain.

   A climbing

   B crossing the road

   C using public transport

4 Frida returned to Mexico from the United States because she _____.

   A held strong political beliefs

   B was in poor health

   C felt homesick

5 Frida says that her paintings were always about the many things she _____.

   A saw

   B felt

   C imagined

4 Draft and redraft a structured email

A student made these notes in preparation for writing an email to a newspaper about improving literacy standards in her country. Use the notes to write the full email.

CB Sections D8 and D9

> Literacy very important: people's happiness & personal development + development of country
>
> Research studies: people unable read/write → more likely dissatisfied with lives + lack confidence + find getting job difficult
>
> In addition: can't help their children (schoolwork) / play active part in community
>
> They find ordinary things difficult (read newspapers / fill in forms)
>
> Many not use internet / social media
>
> Some feel ashamed → cover up problems / pretend can read
>
> Very important these people get help
>
> In our area: literacy scheme → help adults improve reading / writing skills
>
> Schemes like this → help government achieve goal (100 percent literacy our country)

Unit 1: Goals and achievements

Subject: Re: Improving literacy standards

Dear Editor,

....

....

....

....

....

....

....

....

....

....

....

....

....

Yours faithfully,
Vicki Sansa

When you have finished your first draft, check your email carefully and make any corrections that are required.

5 Language study: Apostrophes

CB Section D10

Omission of letters

We use apostrophes to show where letters have been removed. For example, cannot = can't (*n* and *o* have been removed).

Add the missing apostrophes to these sentences.

a   I havent decided what to wear to the party yet.

b   I wish youd be more careful. Youre always breaking things.

c   Shes got a son, Rory, whos nine.

d   Dont you think youd better wear a coat – its raining?

e   Lets meet soon for a coffee. Its ages since Ive seen you.

f   He doesnt know where theyve gone, does he?

g   Arent you hot in that thick sweater?

h   This coffees lost its flavour.

Possession

We use apostrophes to show that something belongs to someone or something. For example, *Latifa's pen* shows that the pen belongs to Latifa (not that letters are missing). We put the apostrophe after the 'owner' if it is plural. For example, *the students' books* shows us that there are several students, not just one.

Add the missing apostrophes to these sentences.

i   Hu Chengs parents carefully read his class teachers report.

j   All three of the sisters cars were repaired in Eddies garage.

k   The students ID cards were checked by the colleges security guard.

l   The politicians listened to all of the peoples opinions.

m   I think womens professional football teams should be paid as much as mens.

n   Alicias cat ran across several of her neighbours gardens.

Add the missing apostrophes of both omission and possession to these sentences.

o   Elenas got two weeks work at the end of July.

p   Ill see you at your sisters wedding.

q   Thats why the boys father was angry with them.

Unit 1: Goals and achievements

r   Its a really long way to the doctors from my house.

s   The girls bedroom was being decorated so she couldnt do her homework there.

t   Shops really cant afford to ignore their customers opinions.

6 Present simple and continuous

CB Grammar spotlight

Complete these sentences using the correct present form of the verb in brackets.

a   I can't believe that Delphine _____ (enjoy) listening to this band – she usually _____ (hate) this kind of music.

b   I _____ (suppose) that Rishab will win the tennis tournament. He _____ (play) really well.

c   Magda and Karolina usually _____ (avoid) talking about politics but they _____ (argue) about it now.

d   I _____ (read) a really good book at the moment, which _____ (contain) lots of information about the history of my country.

e   I _____ not (understand) what this man _____ (say) to me. Can you translate it for me, please?

17

> Unit 2
Fitness and well-being

A What is a healthy lifestyle?

1 Vocabulary check

CB Section A1

Circle the letter of the best option to complete the sentences.

1 It's important to have a _____ diet and not just eat the same thing every day.

   A mixed   B varied   C wide

2 Many people think that having a regular _____ -up at the doctor's is a good idea.

   A check   B test   C examine

3 Some people argue that you don't need vitamin _____ if you have a good diet.

   A supplements   B extras   C additions

4 It's important to avoid eating lots of _____ food, like ready meals and packet soups.

   A managed   B treated   C processed

5 Spending time each day relaxing and doing things you enjoy helps reduce stress _____.

   A totals   B levels   C amounts

6 It's sometimes very difficult to maintain a good work–life _____.

   A mixture   B comparison   C balance

2 Understanding pie charts

Leyfield Leisure Centre analysed the popularity of the activities it offers to users. Study the pie chart, then complete the paragraph.

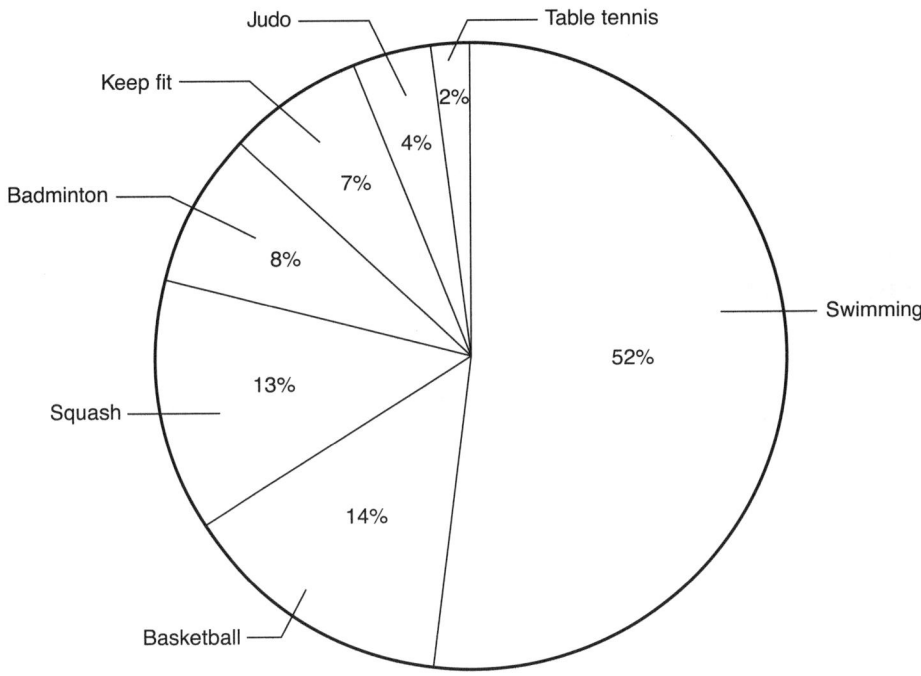

The most popular activity by far is (a) _____ and the least popular is (b) _____.

The second most popular activity is (c) _____.

Over a quarter of users of the leisure centre come to play (d) _____ and squash.

Badminton is only a little ahead of (e) _____ in popularity, but it is twice as popular as (f) _____.

3 Suffixes and spellings

Add a suitable suffix to the words in brackets to complete the sentences.

a   Winning three out of the four races she took part in was quite an _____ (achieve) for Sylvia.

b   Amin said his main _____ (motivate) for learning Japanese was a desire to live in Japan one day.

c   It was a truly _____ (memory) concert, and the audience applauded for a long time at the end.

> CB Section A11 and A12

d There's a huge _____ (diverse) of wildlife in the forest: everything from elephants to exotic birds.

e Rusul was worried about the small stain on his shirt, but it was hardly _____ (notice).

f The tennis player wasn't concentrating and made a _____ (care) mistake when hitting the ball back.

g It's not _____ (advise) to swim in the lake as the water is too cold.

h It was _____ (courage) of Jack to challenge his manager's decision.

B Note-making and sports

1 Note-making practice

Quickly read this article about a kung fu club. Then write notes outlining the practical steps the owner has taken to ensure the club is a success. It is a good idea to underline the relevant points as you read.

CB Section B3

Dan De Sousa is the owner of the successful Fairways Kung Fu Club, now in its second year. The early years were far from easy, though.

Dan admits he was worried at first about the lack of interest from the public. 'The main problem when we started the club,' he explains, 'was the perception of kung fu as an aggressive sport, which can result in serious injuries.'

Parents, in particular, were worried, and the initial take-up of membership was very low. In order to improve understanding of the martial art, Dan ran a social-media campaign pointing out that anyone can learn to do it, whatever their level of fitness or previous experience. Another marketing tool he has used is a video promoting its benefits as a mental discipline that actually increases self-control. He circulates the video to schools and on video-sharing sites and has received some positive feedback. These methods are paying off, and the club is flourishing. Membership is up by 50 percent on last year, and girls as well as boys are becoming converts. Structured training courses have been specially devised for all levels of ability – from those starting from scratch to advanced levels.

Unit 2: Fitness and well-being

> Dan supervises the training and the participants' safety is the first priority. Although some members of the public still believe it encourages aggressive behaviour, there is no doubt that attitudes to kung fu are changing. Furthermore, Dan insists that only friendly competition is allowed. Instructors have to be qualified before he employs them, and also trained in first aid.
>
> Dan has gone to a lot of trouble to redecorate the club house. The attractive cream-and-blue-painted changing rooms are fully equipped with hot showers, hairdryers, lockers and mirrors. 'I want members to feel proud of Fairways and to feel good about coming here,' Dan says.

2 Linking ideas

Complete sentences a–f using endings 1–6. Write the number in the box next to the correct starter phrase.

a   Hassan is a very competitive child and always

b   For children who aren't good at sport, sports day

c   People say that losing at sport isn't bad for children. On the contrary, they

d   It was raining so heavily yesterday that we

e   It was a very close match, and our team

f   I found the sight of so many children crying because they had lost the match

1 very upsetting.
2 has to be on the winning team.
3 can be an annual torment.
4 won by a single goal we scored just before the end.
5 abandoned the idea of swimming in the open-air pool.
6 believe it is character-building.

3 Sentence correction

Each of these sentences contains an incorrect verb form. Identify the mistake, then rewrite the sentence using the correct verb form.

a   When the referee blew the whistle at the end of the game, neither team was scoring a single goal.

   ....

   ....

b   Did you ever won a big competition?

   ....

   ....

c   My bicycle had a puncture today although I was replacing the tyre last week.

   ....

   ....

d   Did Hala told you why she wasn't chosen for the team?

   ....

   ....

e   The child was in tears because he had fell off his bike.

   ....

   ....

Unit 2: Fitness and well-being

f Where have you bought your tennis racket?

....

....

g Dentists are taking care of people's teeth.

....

....

h Last week, I had twisted my ankle playing hockey.

....

....

4 Language study: Measurements as adjectives

CB Section B10

The following pairs of sentences contain one compound adjective that is correct and one that is incorrect. Put a tick (✓) against the correct one and a cross (✗) against the incorrect one. The first one has been done for you.

a He lives in a seven-million-dollar house.   ✓

    She's just bought a 14-bedrooms house.   ✗

b The company was awarded a two-million euro contract.   _____

    The 500-million-pound contract was to provide six new aircraft.   _____

c The 10 000-metre-race was won by an Ethiopian athlete.   _____

    The 3000-kilometre cycling event takes place over three weeks.   _____

d I'm exhausted because I worked a 15-hour shift last night.   _____

    It was a 14-hours-flight to their holiday destination.   _____

e This phone gets lots of five-star review on shopping websites.   _____

    Although it was only a three-star hotel, it was actually quite luxurious.   _____

C Fitness and technology

1 Pre-reading task

Use the words and expressions in the box to complete the definitions.

CB Section C2

> gather dust   enhanced   real-time   simulation   toned
> high-resolution   intention   astonishing   monitor   hooked

a If you have the _____ of doing something, it means you really hope to do it.

b A _____ is a situation, place or event that is made to look real but isn't.

c If something is left to _____, it means it's not used for a long time.

d Something that is _____ is very impressive or surprising.

e If a display is _____ it means it's very clear.

f If you see an event in _____, you watch it as it is taking place.

g If you _____ something, it means you check it carefully over a period of time.

h Something that is _____ is better than it was before.

i If you are _____ on something, it means you can't stop doing it.

j If your body is _____ it means it is very fit after doing lots of exercise.

2 Reading for gist and detail

Quickly read the description of the indoor cycling machine and circle the correct option to answer these questions about the text.

CB Sections C2 and C4

1 The most likely place you would read this text is:

   A in an online review.

   B in a technical report.

   C in publicity material.

2   The cycling machine has many features which make it:

   A   similar to riding a traditional bike.

   B   relatively easy to store at home.

   C   possible to ride virtually with friends.

Tour de France Elite Cycling Machine

Long gone are the days when cycling machines are bought with every good intention, used once or twice and then put into a cupboard or spare room to gather dust. The Tour de France Elite will have you hooked from the first ride and your body toned to perfection in double-quick time.

The bike is designed to feel as much as possible like the real thing, and the hi-tech programming gives you enormous flexibility. Its astonishing range of options allows you to experience in your living room every form of cycling you can think of, from a leisurely weekend ride along the river to competing in a professional road race. The high-resolution screen allows you to see the surrounding countryside passing by as you ride, as well as any other riders and road-users nearby. You can even take part in real-time competitions with your friends on their Tour de France Elites without ever having to leave your home. You can create individual profiles so that every member of the household can save their data and monitor their progress. Available in Standard and Deluxe versions, the latter includes simulations of every professional road race, plus enhanced graphics of the world's best velodromes, for the ultimate Olympic racing experience.

Re-read the text and decide if the statements are true (T), false (F) or doesn't say (DS). Circle your answers.

a   Old cycling machines often weren't used very much.   T / F / DS

b   It takes time to start enjoying the Tour de France Elite.   T / F / DS c   You will probably become fit very quickly using the Tour de France Elite.   T / F / DS

d   The Tour de France Elite uses very little electricity.   T / F / DS

e   You can choose to cycle in lots of different situations on the machine.   T / F / DS

f   The screen doesn't show images particularly clearly.   T / F / DS

g   The Tour de France Elite uses quite a lot of floor space.   T / F / DS

h   You can store several different people's information on the machine.   T / F / DS

i   There are two different models of the Tour de France Elite.   T / F / DS

j   The Tour de France Elite is used by several Olympic athletes.   T / F / DS

3 Pre-listening task

Use the words and phrases in the box to complete the sentences.

> simulated   approaching   unnatural   sort out   struggle
> demonstration   set up   running

a   The computer didn't work because it wasn't _____ properly.

b   The date for the race is getting nearer and nearer – it's _____ fast.

c   Magnus knows lots about technology so he can _____ any problems you have.

d   It was a real _____ getting the machine to work – it took ages!

e   The device wasn't working but I've got it up and _____ now.

f   On the screen, you can cycle through _____ countryside that looks very real.

g   The salesperson gave us a _____ of how the cycling machine worked.

h   The colours on that display are totally _____ – the trees look blue!

Unit 2: Fitness and well-being

 4 Listening for detail and attitude

You will hear four people giving their opinions. Listen and match the opinions below to the speakers. There are two extra opinions you do not need to use.

CB Section C9

Which speaker:

A   has already taken part in some races?

B   wishes they had bought a new bike instead?

C   is impressed by the quality of the display?

D   has felt the benefits of using the machine quite quickly?

E   found the machine difficult to set up?

F   is surprised by how quiet it is?

Speaker 1: _____   Speaker 3: _____

Speaker 2: _____   Speaker 4: _____

What are the speakers all talking about?

....

D Different approaches to well-being

1 Vocabulary check

Circle or underline the correct word from each pair in *italics*.

a   My heart was *beating / banging* so fast, I had to sit down and take deep breaths.

b   The idea of even being able to run more than a few hundred metres was *inconceivable / inconclusive* to Max.

c   Jin gets so *immune / immersed* in his training, he often won't even have a break.

d   Mr Grey says hard work is more of a *key / cue* to success in sport than natural talent.

e   I look and feel better since I started taking walks and getting more *fresh / bright* air and exercise.

f   Children need praise and *enhancement / encouragement* if they are to do well at sport.

g   Alan was so tired after the day's work that he used to *slump / stumble* in front of the TV and do nothing all evening.

h   Sasha wants to get fit and has booked a *consultation / confrontation* with a personal trainer.

i   I got an eye injury when I was playing tennis and it is in *fear / danger* of becoming infected.

j   Do you think the new football captain has enough experience to *bring / take* command of the team?

2 Pre-reading task

You are going to read three short articles in which different people give their opinions about 'superfoods'. Answer these questions before you read the articles.

CB Sections D2 and D3

a   Why might some foods be described as 'superfoods'?

   ....

   ....

b   What benefits do you think superfoods might give you?

   ....

   ....

c   What kind of foods do you think superfoods might be?

   ....

   ....

Draw lines to match the words to their definitions.

a   fad   designed to make people believe something that is not true

b   miraculous   a member of the public who buys goods or services

c   misleading   certainly

d   alarm   to argue or disagree about something

e   consumer   a fashion that is only popular for a short time

f   fuss   to cause worry of fear

g   dispute   an unnecessary show of excitement or concern

h   undoubtedly   something positive that is hard to believe or explain

3 Reading

Read the article about superfoods, then write numbers in the boxes to answer the questions.

CB Section D4

Superfoods: fact or fad?

Most people who have even the slightest interest in health and diet have come across so-called 'superfoods'. Although there is no scientific definition of what a superfood is, many people claim that certain fruits, nuts, fish, vegetables and spices offer almost miraculous benefits to health, and therefore have earned the title of superfood. But are these claims actually true? We asked three people involved in diet and health for their opinions.

1 **Angela Helmswick PhD, senior researcher in dietary health**

While there is little doubt that what are generally referred to as superfoods have health benefits, research suggests that some of the claims made about them are, at best, misleading and, at worst, may actually be dangerous. Rightly or wrongly, many people are keen to believe that there is something they can eat that provides the solution to all of their health problems or concerns. While they may encourage healthy eating for many, what alarms many experts is that certain consumers may base their diet almost entirely on superfoods and therefore miss out on the essential nutrients that other foods contain but superfoods do not.

2 **Martin Trotter, independent dietician**

I can't see what's so controversial about superfoods, and dispute the claims that suggest they are no more beneficial for health than many other foods – the health benefits have been scientifically proven again and again. Why is it so hard to believe that some foods might be better for us than others? I agree to an extent that superfoods have been overused on the packaging of some food products in order to sell more of them, and that food companies use the image of superfoods to keep prices high for products containing them. However, that kind of practice has been going on for years, with manufacturers only too keen to point out that their cereal or ready meal is high in vitamins and minerals.

3 **Amina Begum, consumer adviser, *Food Health magazine***

Superfoods really are a marketing executive's dream, and labels on food products claiming to be packed full of various superfoods are now hard to miss! It's a shame in a way, as what have become known as superfoods are undoubtedly amazingly good for you, but presenting them as capable of preventing or even curing some really quite serious illnesses is totally unhelpful! I suppose they do allow people to discover some wonderfully delicious new foods, but my fear is that consumers will focus overly on foods containing them when in fact by far the healthiest diet you can have is one that's packed with every possible food type.

Which person:

a   says that claims about healthy ingredients on food products are nothing new? ☐

b   shares Angela Helmswick's view that superfoods can cause health problems? ☐

c   suggests that consumers believe things that may not be true to reduce their fears? ☐

d   agrees with Martin Trotter that superfoods are frequently mentioned on food products? ☐

4 Style and features

Read the article about superfoods again, then write numbers in the boxes to answer these questions about the features of the text.

CB Section D7

Which person:

a   uses a rhetorical question to make the text sound more interesting? ☐

b   uses words like 'may' and 'research suggests' to show that even experts are not 100 percent certain? ☐

c   tends to use exciting words and exclamation marks to make the text sound more appealing? ☐

d   uses the most formal language? ☐

e   avoids giving their personal opinion? ☐

5 Note-taking and article-writing

Make notes about the positive and negative aspects of superfoods mentioned in the article.

CB Section D9 and D10

Positive aspects	Negative aspects

The three writers do not agree on some points. Use the information in the article, and your own research online, to write a short article presenting your own opinions about superfoods.

Make sure you use interesting vocabulary, avoid repeating words or phrases, and join clauses and ideas together to create complex sentences. For example:

Certain types of foods are known as superfoods. Many people believe they are very healthy. Other people disagree. ✗

So-called superfoods are thought by many people to be extremely healthy, although others disagree. ✓

6 Sentence correction: Zero, first and second conditionals

CB Grammar spotlight

Remember the structure of zero, first and second conditionals:

Zero conditional: *If* + subject + present tense, subject + present tense
(*If I drink* coffee, *I can't* sleep.)

Zero conditionals are used for something that is *always true*.

First conditional: *If* + subject + present tense, subject + future form
(*If it rains*, *you'll get* wet.)

First conditionals are used for something that is *likely to happen*.

Second conditional: *If* + subject + past tense, subject + *would* + main verb
(*If it snowed* in summer, *I would be* surprised.)

Second conditionals are used for something that is *possible, but not likely*.

Insert the missing word in the right place in each of these sentences.

a   If the weather hot, ice cream melts very quickly.

b   If I won a million dollars, I buy a really nice house.

c   If it rains a lot, the cricket match be cancelled.

d   I met someone famous, I wouldn't know what to say.

e   Plants die if they not get enough water.

f   If the racket doesn't cost too much, I buy it.

g   If I lived close to a lake or the sea, I would swimming every day.

h   Sergio's parents are to be so pleased if Sergio wins the tournament.

> Unit 3
Where we live

A Our neighbourhood

1 Forming open questions

CB Section A1

Rewrite these closed questions to make them open.

a   Have you lived in your neighbourhood for a long time?

   ....

b   Have there been any changes?

   ....

c   Do you like growing up there?

   ....

d   Do you have nice friends?

   ....

e   Do you belong to a club?

   ....

f   Are there places to spend free time near you?

   ....

Now write down how you would answer each of these open questions.

a   ....
b   ....
c   ....
d   ....

e ....

f ....

2 Pre-reading task

Replace the words and phrases in *italics* in the sentences with a word from the box.

> transform   affordable   adequate   worn-out   investment
> renovated   do up   scandalous

a   I bought an old house in a terrible condition which I'm going to *improve*.   _____

b   There are very few houses that are *cheap enough* for those on low incomes.   _____

c   I need a new jacket because this one is really *old and damaged*.   _____

d   The suggested improvements to the park are really going to *change* it.   _____

e   The old theatre has been *made as good as new* and it looks fantastic now.   _____

f   The public transport in this town isn't *good enough*.   _____

g   I think it's *terrible* that the council has made so few improvements.   _____

h   There needs to be a lot more *money spent* in this part of the city.   _____

3 Reading letters

Read the extracts from letters that three residents have written to their local newspaper about improvements they would like to see in their neighbourhoods. Match the questions to the residents. You will need to write each resident's number more than once.

Which resident:

a   thinks that litter is a major problem in the area?   ☐

b   would like to see increased investment in affordable housing?   ☐

c   says there should be more forms of entertainment in the area? ☐

d   believes that many of the roads in their area need repairing? ☐

e   wants more jobs to be available in the local area? ☐

f   hasn't noticed any improvements being made at all recently? ☐

g   thinks the public transport in their area is reasonably good? ☐

h   would like a local park to be renovated? ☐

> **1 Fernando**
>
> I love living in this area but nowhere is perfect, of course. While the connections to other parts of the city via bus and train links are more than adequate, there just isn't enough to do here for adults, children or young people. Other areas have set up community-owned cinemas and other projects with the help of the local council, and I think it's totally possible to do similar things here. On the plus side, plenty has been spent on rental accommodation that even less well-off families can afford, and the park's been transformed from something resembling a giant green litter bin into a really pleasant, clean area to do a bit of exercise. I think the council should try to attract a greater number of businesses into the area, though, as there aren't very many employment opportunities in the neighbourhood at the moment.
>
> **2 Asha**
>
> I've lived here for 20 years now and think a lot needs doing to improve the area. While there seemed to be something being done more or less every week previously – replacing worn-out roads and that kind of thing – nothing's been happening in the last few weeks and months, at least that I've seen. The cost of renting or buying a home here these days is scandalous. The only way most people will ever be able to move here is if lots more houses and homes are built that are in a price range that makes them accessible to those on average or low incomes. There's only one green space in the neighbourhood, which is really popular. I know it's impossible to create more parks out of nowhere, but the council should prioritise doing up the one we've got, as the paths and play equipment are looking a bit sad.

> **3 Kim**
>
> I moved to this area when I got a job here a year or so ago and think it's a great place, but it has lots of potential to get even better. I cycle whenever I can rather than taking my car. That's partly to help the environment but also because it's so much quicker than using public transport. Hardly any buses come close to where I live these days so I just don't bother. Anyway, I've noticed that the state of most of the streets here is shameful. I almost fell off my bike the other day after I hit a huge hole. Something really needs to be done about it. I must say that I've never been short of things to do here – there's a cinema, leisure centre, theatre and even an ice rink. However, I wish the council would provide more bins and employ more people to pick up all the rubbish that people throw away.

Read the letter extracts again and do these tasks.

a   Tick (✓) the statement that best explains the purpose of the first sentence in each of the letter extracts.

    A   It summarises the writer's opinion about the neighbourhood.   _____

    B   It explains how the writer came to live in the neighbourhood.   _____

    C   It gives details of the writer's main concern about the neighbourhood.   _____

b   What features do the writers use to support their points? Tick (✓) all that apply.

    A   Information   _____

    B   Examples   _____

    C   Explanations   _____

c   In each letter extract, 1, 2 and 3, underline examples where the writer mentions something positive about the area in one sentence then contrasts it with a problem in the next.

4 Colloquial language

Circle the best meaning for each of the expressions in *italics*.

CB Section A4

1   'I'm trying to learn the clarinet but it's really difficult.' 'You need to *give it time.*'

    A   be patient

    B   practise more often

    C   wait until you're older

2   Anna says she doesn't like her new manager at work, but *it's early days*.

   A   Her new manager is less experienced than she is.

   B   She doesn't like starting work before 9 a.m.

   C   She may change her mind when she knows the manager better.

3   When I fell off my bike and broke my leg, my dad was *my rock*.

   A   very hard on me

   B   very supportive

   C   very upset

4   Fatima is lucky to find such a good job *on her doorstep*.

   A   next door to where she lives

   B   in her immediate neighbourhood

   C   doing work from home

5   We're all *going for a bite to eat* before the film.

   A   buying food from a street seller

   B   having a light meal of some kind

   C   cooking a barbecue

6   Liam wants to leave school without taking any exams, but his parents have *dug their heels in* over it.

   A   had terrible arguments

   B   refused to change their mind

   C   talked to the teachers

5 Language study: Using the gerund

CB Section A5

Use a verb from the box to complete the sentences. Make sure you use the correct form of the verb. There is one extra verb that you do not need to use.

| have   stay   send   miss   see   wait   do |

a   I'm really looking forward to _____ you at the weekend.

b   Stefania felt really tired after _____ up so late the previous night.

c   _____ exercise first thing every morning is a great way to start the day.

d   Leave now or you'll risk _____ your train!

e   I don't think I'll ever get used to Marlon _____ a beard – he looks so strange!

f   Smitri got fed up of _____ for Virender to arrive so she left.

B Living in different locations

1 Choose the best word

Circle the letter of the correct word to complete each sentence.

1   People often prefer living in new houses as the _____ costs are usually lower than in old buildings.

   A support   B maintenance   C repairing   D developing

2   Long-distance buses may have toilet _____ on them.

   A equipment   B resources   C facilities   D rooms

3   We worked out a(n) _____ for our holiday so we knew how much we could afford to spend each day.

   A budget   B allowance   C account   D savings

4   The bookshop on the high street has closed down and the _____ is/are up for sale.

   A commerce   B premises   C belongings   D trade

5   The children were completely _____ and refused to do what the teacher told them.

   A disorganised   B displeased   B undisciplined   D unpleasant

6   The manager plans to _____ the project after six months to see if the money being spent on it is worthwhile.

   A respond   B review   C recall   D report

7   A _____ restaurant like the Delhi Brasserie deserves to be successful.

   A well-fed   B well-run   C well-balanced   D well-made

8   We didn't think it was right to build a supermarket in the middle of a quiet _____ street.

   A residential   B regional   C community   D urban

9   I would have liked a white sofa and white armchairs for the living room, but as our children are very small, we decided the idea was _____

   A imperfect   B impersonal   C impossible   D impractical

10 Everdale United supporters became very _____ when their team won the match.

   A rowdy   B disturbing   C loudly   D racket

Unit 3: Where we live

2 Pre-listening task

Draw lines to match the meanings of these words to their definitions.

a   security   comfortable and pleasant because it is small and warm

b   throughout   a rounded roof on a building

c   maintenance   a person who designs buildings

d   cosy   in every part of something or during the whole period of time

e   ant   someone who enters another person's property without permission

f   architect   someone or something that gives you ideas for doing something

g   trespasser   protection of people and buildings against dangers

h   dome   the quality of being hard and strong

i   solidity   a small insect that lives in colonies, often underground

j   inspiration   work needed to keep buildings, machines, etc. in good condition

 ## 3 Listening comprehension

You will hear part of an interview with Jamila Balicki, whose home is partly underground. Listen, then circle the letter of the best option for each question.

1   What gave Jamila the idea of building her home partly underground?

   A   watching a nature programme

   B   talking to an architect

   C   seeing pictures in a magazine

2   What surprised Jamila when she first moved into her home?

   A   how much room there was

   B   having lots of natural light

   C   the lack of noise there

3   Compared to Jamila's previous house, her underground home is

   A   more solid, and has more people passing by outside.

   B   bigger, and has about the same amount of light.

   C   damper, and has more places for storing food.

4   What does Jamila say is the biggest advantage of her home?

   A   It makes her feel close to nature.

   B   She feels very safe when she's in it.

   C   It requires very little maintenance.

5   Jamila recently had a problem with

   A   flooding.

   B   insects.

   C   trespassers.

6   Jamila feels that living underground is

   A   not so different to being in a traditional home.

   B   something she's glad she's tried but will soon give up.

   C   generally positive but not without its difficulties.

C Describing places and belongings

1 Order of adjectives

The adjectives in *italics* in these sentences have all been mixed up! Rewrite the sentences so the order is correct. Remember that in English, adjectives follow a particular order:

opinion → size → age → shape → colour → origin → material → purpose → noun

CB Section C1

a   Santiago met a *young Russian tall* at the business meeting.

   ....

b   I accidentally left a *sports leather green medium-sized* bag on the bus this morning.

   ....

c   The *round Italian old beautiful* painting that Pierre bought was a present for his wife.

   ....

Unit 3: Where we live

d Olivia bought a *wooden large dining rectangular modern* table for her new home.

....

e The statue looked like a *plastic green strange long* vegetable!

....

2 Developing your writing style

Rewrite this description in a more interesting way.

CB Section C2

> I have my own bedroom. There is a window in the bedroom. From the window you can see the garden. There is a walnut tree in the garden. The tree is close to my window. I can pick nuts from the tree. My favourite thing in my bedroom is my bed. It is comfortable. It is soft. It has many cushions. There is a bedspread. The bedspread is nice. It is from India. It is silk. The colours of the bedspread are very nice. They are not bright. They are kind of dull colours. I read on my bed. I dream on my bed. My bedroom has a good atmosphere.

....

....

....

....

....

....

....

3 Word formation

Read the article that a student has written for a magazine. To fill each gap, choose a word from the box and change it into the correct form. The first one has been done as an example.

> inspiration   lightly   convert   reduce   ~~swim~~   charming
> relaxation   tradition   owner

A breath of fresh air

My town has lots going for it – parks, a **(a)** <u>swimming</u> pool and several museums. One place, however, has become a definite favourite of mine. Recently, a shop and café, Trade Winds, has opened in a **(b)** _____ warehouse only five minutes away from the centre of town.

The people who **(c)** _____ the shop used to live in Africa, and they import things from all over that continent. You can buy **(d)** _____ handmade jewellery, paintings, gifts and pottery. You can browse for as long as you want. It's the kind of place where no one minds how long you stay or forces you to buy anything. Every now and then, there is a half-price sale with genuine **(e)** _____, which is a bonus if you are on a tight budget.

Trade Winds has a wonderful, **(f)** _____ atmosphere, and upstairs the café is warm and friendly too. I often visit the shop at weekends and meet my friends in the café for some hot chocolate or a **(g)** _____ snack. We can laugh and talk and forget our everyday problems for a while. Trade Winds has brought new life into the community.

Our town still retains an old-world **(h)** _____, but new people and new ideas keep it an enjoyable and **(i)** _____ place to live.

Unit 3: Where we live

D Welcoming an exchange visitor

1 Improving the tone of an email

Rewrite this email to an exchange visitor. Improve its style and use a more welcoming tone. Make sure you use a suitable opening and closing sentence.

CB Section D4

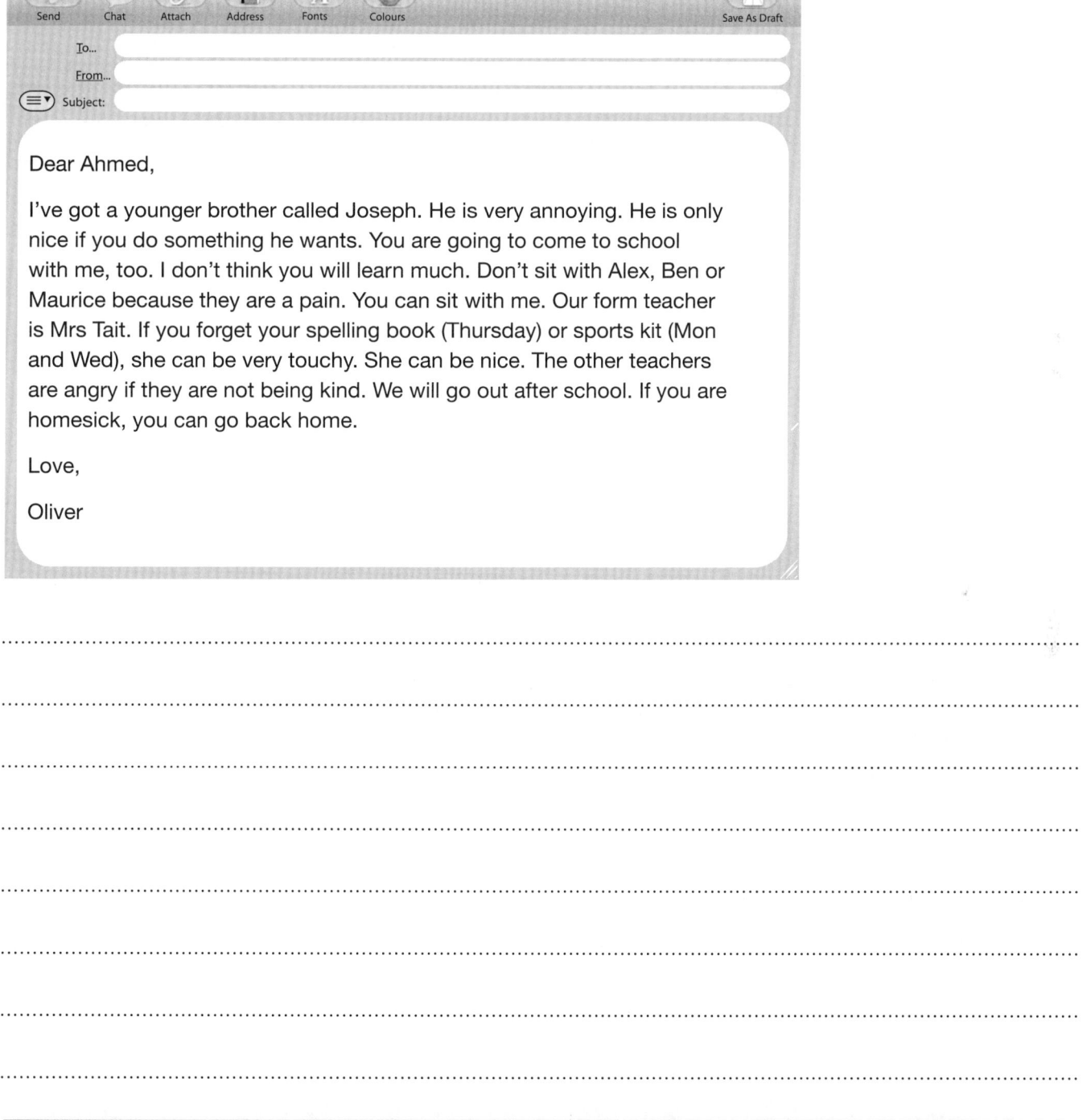

Dear Ahmed,

I've got a younger brother called Joseph. He is very annoying. He is only nice if you do something he wants. You are going to come to school with me, too. I don't think you will learn much. Don't sit with Alex, Ben or Maurice because they are a pain. You can sit with me. Our form teacher is Mrs Tait. If you forget your spelling book (Thursday) or sports kit (Mon and Wed), she can be very touchy. She can be nice. The other teachers are angry if they are not being kind. We will go out after school. If you are homesick, you can go back home.

Love,

Oliver

2 Writing an email

List all the things you think are important when writing an email.

CB Section D9

....

....

....

....

....

....

....

Write an email in response to this task.

An exchange student called Isabel was supposed to be coming to stay with you and your family next month. Unfortunately, you have some problems at home which mean you will have to postpone the visit.

Write an email to Isabel.

In your email:

- apologise for having to postpone the visit
- explain why the visit will have to be postponed
- suggest another time when Isabel could come.

....

....

3 Understanding information in a table

Study this table, which gives details about families offering study holidays for teenagers. The student lives with the family and is taught English at home by one of the parents, who is also a teacher.

Family name	Number of hours of tuition per day	Type of home and local area	Other languages apart from English	Children in family	Pets	Leisure programme
Carter	4–5 hours	Terraced house in suburbs	None	Toddler 2 years; Girl 10 years	Cat	Photography, shopping, cinema
Khan	3–4 hours	Central city flat	Punjabi	Baby 6 months	None	Bowling, museums, theatre, concerts

Family name	Number of hours of tuition per day	Type of home and local area	Other languages apart from English	Children in family	Pets	Leisure programme
Coulden	6 hours	Bungalow in seaside location	French	Twins 18 years	None	Surfing, swimming, fishing
Bloome	7–8 hours	Cottage in large village	None	Baby 10 months; Girl 13 years	Kitten, parrot	Cycling, basketball, walking
Morel	6–8 hours	Large house in town	None	Boy 4 years, Girl 12 years	Hamster, rabbit	Cookery, sewing, computer games, TV
Williams	4 hours	Dairy farm in remote rural area	French	Boy 17 years, Girl 19 years	Horse, kitten	Horse riding, walking
Lilkova	2 hours	Village near sea	Lithuanian	Girl 11 years	Cat	Birdwatching, cycling, boating

Write the name of the family you would choose for each student.

a A Chinese boy of 17 who would like to be in a coastal environment and to be in a family with teenagers of a similar age. _____

b A French girl of 16 and her brother of 17 who prefer indoor activities and require lessons for most of the day. _____

c Twin boys from Norway, aged 16 years old, who want lessons for about 3.5 hours in the morning or afternoon and enjoy watching films in the evening. _____

d A 14-year-old Danish girl who would prefer an urban environment and is allergic to cats. _____

e An 18-year-old French-speaking boy from the Seychelles who loves animals and would like the chance to speak his mother tongue sometimes. _____

f A 14-year-old Mexican boy who loves the beach and the countryside and wants lessons for a couple of hours per day. _____

g A 19-year-old girl who likes the countryside but does not want to live in an isolated environment. _____

Unit 3: Where we live

4 Passives

Remember that all passive forms have the same basic structure: subject + *to be* + past participle. The tense of the verb changes but the structure remains the same. Be careful to use the past participle, not the past simple form – these are not always the same!

CB Grammar spotlight

Correct the mistakes in the sentences.

a   Their new house was much bigger than the old one and is built in 1924.

b   Many more bus routes are planning, both into and out of the city centre.

c   A book describing the history of the town has been wrote by Daniel Rickman.

d   A bridge first constructed across the river as long ago as 1482.

e   The first houses in the new estate will be finish in around six months' time.

f   The product is been advertised online and on television at the moment.

Unit 4
Our impact on the planet

A Global warming and industry

1 Choose the best word

Circle or underline the best option from each pair in *italics*.

CB Section A1

a   Every industry has a negative effect *against / on* the environment, but some create more problems than others.

b   Many millions of *garments / costumes*, such as dresses, shirts and trousers, are produced every year.

c   People can cut down their *carbon footprint / global warming* by buying fewer clothes.

d   Many clothes aren't *planned / designed* to last long and so are thrown away within a year of being bought.

e   The fashion industry has a much *greater / heavier* effect on the environment than most people imagine.

f   The burning of petroleum and other *greenhouse gases / fossil fuels* is a major contributor to global warming.

g   If clothes are a blend of different *materials / resources*, it is much more difficult to recycle them.

h   Many *clients / consumers* in richer nations buy far more clothes each year than they actually need.

2 Reading: Scanning practice

The following leaflet was written by students for motorists and is aimed at making their town a better place to live. Scan the text to find the answers to these questions.

CB Section A6

a   Which illness is mentioned in the text?

   ....

b   What reason is given for more students not walking to school?

   ....

c   How many people does the writer think fast drivers might hurt?

   ....

Unit 4: Our impact on the planet

d What suggestion does the writer make for helping wildlife?

....

e What kinds of cars does the writer suggest that motorists should get?

....

> **Speeding drivers**
> There are a lot of dangerous drivers around here and the culprit is you! You get up late on Monday, don't have time for breakfast, and tear through the town breaking the speed limit. You could injure half a dozen students on their way to school! Thirty-three percent of us now come to school by car. More of us would walk to school if the roads weren't so dangerous, so please slow down!
>
> **Car fumes**
> Are you driving a fuel-efficient model? When you need a new car, do you even consider getting an electric car or a hybrid? It's not just school pupils who are suffering from asthma – so are adults. Reducing car fumes will mean cleaner air for everyone.
>
> **Park and Ride**
> The 'Park and Ride' system means you can now leave your car outside town and get to the centre quickly using the bus. No one likes sitting in traffic jams, so why aren't you using it?
>
> **Wildlife**
> Driving contributes to pollution, which is harmful to people and to wildlife too. You can help protect our birds and wild creatures by not making unnecessary journeys by car.

3 Vocabulary check

Using the information from the text in the coursebook, add the missing letters to the incomplete words in these sentences.

CB Section A7

a I never shop in up _ _ _ _ _ t clothes shops because they're too expensive.

b Some b _ _ _ _ _ _ _ _ s from food crops can be used to creating clothing and fuel instead of being thrown away.

c A m _ _ _ d is used to make the shoes to ensure they have the correct shape.

d More and more companies are making clothes from d _ _ _ _ s that's washed up on beaches, like old fishing nets.

e   Creating clothing using a range of recycled materials found in the sea was the

    b _ _ _ _ _ _ _ _ d of EcoALF company founder Javier Goyeneche.

f   Many researchers are investigating a more environmentally friendly

    s _ _ _ _ _ _ _ _ e for plastic bottles.

4 Language study: Using connectives to guide the readers

CB Section A9

Because is used to give reasons. It joins an action or event to the reason for it, so you don't usually start a new sentence with because. *Since* or *as* can sometimes be used instead of because, and these words can be used to begin a sentence.

Example: *People were afraid of travelling by train because/since/as they thought it could cause health problems.*

Not: *People were afraid of travelling by train. Because/Since/As they thought it could cause health problems.*

Use *because*, *since* or *as* to make complete sentences from these prompts.

a   roads getting more crowded / number cars manufactured / increasing

    ....

b   parents not allow me / have motorcycle / too dangerous

    ....

c   swimming lessons cancelled / pool leaking

    ....

d   train travel became more popular / safety checks / introduced

    ....

As a result of / Therefore / That's why are all used to express the consequence of something.

Example: *Railways enabled people to travel around the country more easily. As a result, their employment opportunities increased.*

So means the same but is more informal. You do not usually start a new sentence with *so*.

Example: *It started to rain so we decided to stay at home.*

Unit 4: Our impact on the planet

Write a consequence for each of these sentences. Use the prompts in brackets and one of the expressions above.

a   The pilot told passengers that the fog was too thick to risk landing in London. (*land / Manchester*)

    ....

b   There is a great deal of pressure to look good nowadays. (*feel inadequate*)

    ....

c   Several new companies have opened up in our town. (*house prices / rise*)

    ....

d   Marian's ticket was out of date. (*buy / new one*)

    ....

A writer may use linking expressions such as *In addition, Furthermore, What's more* and *as well* to add extra information.

Example: *The volunteers filled over 100 big bags with trash found on the beach. In addition, / Furthermore, / What's more, they removed 500 kg of larger items such as discarded fishing nets.*
OR *They removed 500 kg of larger items such as discarded fishing nets as well.*

Add a new sentence to each of the following, using the prompts in brackets. Use one of the linking words or phrases above.

a   Cars produce a lot of pollution. (*relatively / dangerous / form of transport*)

    ....

b   Growing cotton takes up a lot of land which could be used to produce food. (*large amounts / water / require / grow well*)

    ....

c   A large petrol company has decided not to open a petrol station in the village because the population is small and people's incomes are low. (*most use bikes / get / work*)

    ....

d We were disappointed with our day out to the theme park. The tickets cost a lot of money and you had to pay extra for some of the attractions. (*long queues / get on rides / some rides not working*)

....

e If a factory were built in our village, young people would no longer have to leave the area to look for work. (*factory / encourage more people / move into village / as a result / local shops / get more customers*)

....

5 Understanding graphs

Study the chart showing ticket sales of two airlines, Sunair and Easyfly. Then answer the questions.

> CB International overview

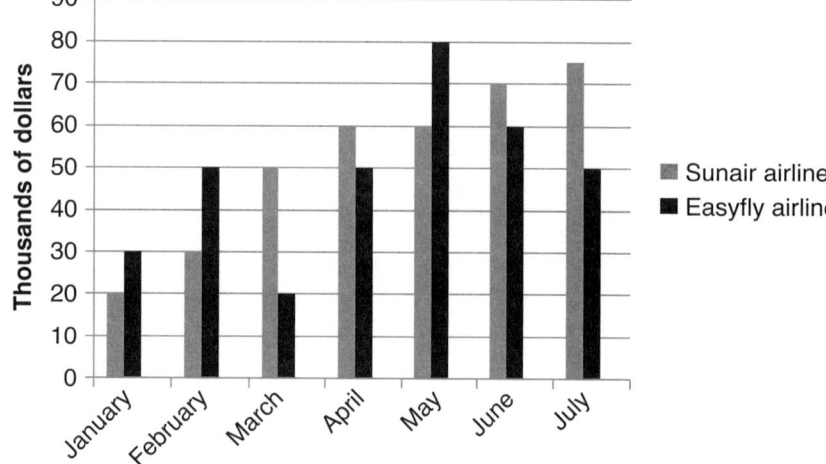

a What was the value of Easyfly sales in February? _____

b In which month did Easyfly sales drop sharply? _____

c How much was earnt from Sunair sales in June? _____

d What was the best month for Easyfly sales? _____

e Is the trend for Sunair sales up or down? _____

Unit 4: Our impact on the planet

B Transport

1 Pre-listening task

Draw lines to match these words to the correct definition.

a   matter   a disadvantage or problem

b   harmful   to show something in public for the first time

c   drawback   in a gradual but increasing way

d   project   a physical substance

e   progressively   to estimate using information already known

f   unveil   able to damage something or someone

2 Listening task: Hydrogen, the fuel of the future?

CB Section B3

Listen to a scientist giving a talk about using a gas called hydrogen as an environmentally friendly fuel. Complete the notes below.

a   _____ percent of everything in the universe is made of hydrogen.

b   One disadvantage is that it's _____ to produce.

c   The global market in hydrogen may be worth

    $_____ trillion by 2050.

d   Some public transport, planes and _____ will probably be powered by hydrogen one day.

e   Airbus hopes to have a hydrogen-powered

    plane running by _____.

f   The plane will be able to carry _____ people.

3 Euphemisms

Add one extra word to each of these sentences to complete the euphemisms.

a   I think she's being economical with the _____, so I don't believe her!

b   Unfortunately, our next-door neighbour passed _____ yesterday at the age of 90.

c   Their car had seen better _____ and looked as though it might break down any minute

d   My grandparents can get 50 percent off all rail travel with a Senior _____ Rail Card.

e   Alison is _____ jobs at the moment so if you see any good work opportunities, let her know.

f   Max is very _____ with his money, so pays for as little as possible when we go out together.

C Looking for solutions

1 Paragraphing and punctuation

Rewrite this report to a school management committee, adding the correct punctuation and paragraphing. Don't forget to read it through first to get the sense.

> at the end of the spring term our class held a fundraising barbecue we decided after some disagreement to donate the funds to the local hospital some students argued that the school needed the money to help replace our classroom laptops however in my opinion we made the right decision to donate the money to a good cause although organising the event was hard work and time-consuming I think most of us enjoyed selling the tickets and cooking the food in addition the nurses told us our donation helped to buy oxygen cylinders for emergency use which made us feel very proud the majority of us agreed saving lives is more important than state-of-the-art computers nevertheless a few students disagreed and I understand their point of view in conclusion I think that although most of our fundraising efforts should continue to benefit local charities we should have one event each year just for our school if the headteacher gives permission perhaps we could use the money we raise to have our classroom computers replaced please let me know if you require any further information about our fundraising activities and plans
>
> *Jordan Inara*
>
> Student representative to the school management committee

CB Section B5

Unit 4: Our impact on the planet

2 Presenting the pros and cons

There is a proposal to build a factory in a beautiful area of countryside. A resident, Paula, has written to the local paper putting forward the pros and cons of the idea. Match the *italic* words and phrases in her email with the following headings. Two have been done as examples.

> CB Sections C7 and C8

Listing In the first place

Contrast _____

Reasoning _____

Emphasis _____

Addition _____

Consequence I was delighted

Opinion _____

Summing up _____

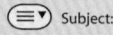 Subject:

Dear Editor,

I was delighted when I heard of the proposal to build a new furniture factory *because* we really need more jobs in this area. If a factory were built in Kemble, our economic future would be secure, and young people *in particular* would no longer have to leave the area to look for work. I realise there are a number of problems concerned with the proposal *but* these could be overcome.

In the first place, it has been pointed out that there is no access road to the site where the proposed factory would be built. *In my view, however,* a new road to the factory could be constructed by cutting through the wood that surrounds the village.

Secondly, the factory would encourage more people to move into Kemble, resulting in increased pressure on housing. *However*, a block of flats could be built on the edge of the village, where the recreation ground is now. *Therefore*, I think the overcrowding objection can be answered.

Another point to consider is that a bigger population has many advantages. The village shop would have more customers, for example. *As a result*, it could expand and offer a better range of goods. *Moreover*, the local school would get more pupils. *Consequently*, more teachers would be recruited and better resources would probably be made available.

In conclusion, I think we should definitely go ahead with the new factory *as surely* all these advantages outweigh any disadvantages that people might be concerned about.

Yours faithfully,

Paula Marconi

Unit 4: Our impact on the planet

3 Language study: Further connectives

CB Section C9

The following text is part of a school newsletter article. Complete each section in the most appropriate way. Write the letter of the best option in the box.

Do you ever get fed up with tripping over bits of wire and old drinks cans, and bumping into joggers while you are trying to enjoy playing a game of basketball? Well, I've got good news for you! The council has offered us some money for a new recreation area. It's going to be properly surfaced and provided with benches and a shelter. ☐

A Nevertheless, joggers will probably object to the idea.

B There is no doubt that these improvements will benefit everyone.

C Moreover, we will have to raise some of the funds ourselves.

The new area will be open to anyone who wants to use it. ☐

D Consequently, we can play safely without scrambling over weeds or broken glass.

E On the other hand, crying babies in their pushchairs will no longer be in the way.

F Undoubtedly, it will be extremely popular, especially with teenagers.

I welcome the decision to improve the recreation area in the local park rather than the Old People's Centre. ☐

G In particular, I am delighted that, for once, young people have been the main consideration.

H So unfortunately the old people will have to wait quite a long time for better facilities.

I Moreover, teenagers will take good care of their new facility.

4 Text completion

CB Section C11

Read this school magazine article about water scarcity and think of one suitable word to fill each gap.

I decided to write for the school magazine **(a)** _____ I am really upset about the way some people take water for granted.

I wonder if you have ever been really, really thirsty? So thirsty that you **(b)** _____ drink dirty water? Have you ever known the kind of thirst that makes your tongue feel swollen in your mouth and cracks your lips? Hmm! I thought not! Water scarcity is not a subject that troubles many of us.

The next time you dive into the school swimming pool, I would like you to think about Jay, who faces water scarcity every day. I made friends **(c)** _____ Jay over the internet when our class did a project on climate change. Mrs Dara, who taught us geography, formed a partnership with a school in Uganda. Jay and I have **(d)** _____ emailing each other ever since.

Each morning, Jay has to walk for an hour to fetch water, **(e)** _____ her family then use for cooking and drinking. Carrying water home from the well may make her late for school, **(f)** _____ Jay never complains. In fact, she thinks she is lucky. She says her uncle has a farm in another part of Uganda **(g)** _____ there has been a drought for two years.

I was so delighted **(h)** _____ Jay emailed to say a new irrigation system was being installed for local farms that would mean a much better harvest and enough water for her uncle's cattle.

I'm sure you would like to make a difference, so visit our fundraising cake stall on Friday 17th. All the proceeds from our delicious cakes are going to a water charity **(i)** _____ helps build wells in dry areas.

(j) _____, I would like to share these wonderful words from my favourite poet, W. H. Auden: 'Thousands have lived without love, not one without water.'

Unit 4: Our impact on the planet

D The community's views

1 Relating to your target audience

CB Section D7

Read the extracts below and then write a letter in each box to match the extracts with the following target audiences.

A   In our business, we always put our customers first. If you share this approach, please get in touch as we have a number of exciting career openings now available.

B   It was wonderful hearing about life on your farm. You may think looking after the animals is a bit dull, but I'd love to change places with you.

C   Cinemas, sports events, concerts . . . This database is full of invaluable information. Once registered with the site, you'll receive regular e-news, bringing you up-to-date with the latest special offers.

D   We have noticed that a number of people, when dropping their children off at school or collecting them, are driving out along the 'in' road for a quick getaway. This is dangerous, so please keep to the one-way system.

E   I love fashion, but I think there's too much pressure on young people to buy the latest styles. Every month, we read articles like yours, which insist that a new style is in and the outfit we bought last season is out.

F   A number of rumours have been circulating about the proposed developments in the area. I hope that the meeting will allow each homeowner to be better informed about the situation.

Internet users ☐   Residents ☐

Teenage magazine reader ☐   People looking for a job ☐

Parents ☐   A penfriend ☐

2 Writing a balanced report

CB Section D9

Here is an informal text about a class visit to an alternative energy centre. Select the necessary information and write a balanced report in an impersonal style about the class visit for your teacher.

Remember to include:

- a short introduction
- paragraphs mentioning the positive and negative aspects of the trip
- a short conclusion.

Use a formal tone and register. Delete any unnecessary content.

The trip to the alternative energy centre was cool and everyone was like happy, except for Katya, my best friend. The bits of paper they gave us in these cool talks we went to first got lost. Then we saw films about wind power and saving energy. Some of us couldn't see properly and the stuff they gave us there got lost. Loads of us didn't bring folders or nothing to store all this stuff they kept giving to us and some of it got dropped on the floor and left around and in the toilets. Katya really minded losing hers cos she said that the papers with all the facts on was really good and we need it for science. Katya moans at everything. Someone dropped an ice cream on her skirt and she nearly cried but I told her, we are having a day out and we are missing geography and maths, and can eat sweets on the bus home. We went to this amazing gift shop and we all bought lots of cool gifts and stuff. All recycled but well expensive! All I could afford was a necklace made of recycled bottletops. We came back on the bus, and everyone was laughing and joking cos we had such a good time and learnt loads of stuff to help us with our work. But then the bus broke down and it took hours to fix so we got back later. Anyway, everyone was saying we are never gonna waste energy again and we are gonna be more careful in future, which has gotta be good for this planet. And I'm definitely gonna have solar panels when I am older. Do you have solar panels? And we just can't wait to get to go again. They told us it is the best in the country. You did a good job sending us there! Thanks a million! Bye for now!

Unit 4: Our impact on the planet

3 Making predictions

There is one mistake in each of the sentences below. Correct the mistakes.

CB Grammar spotlight

a   Local authorities have said that it likely the town will be flooded soon.

b   Energy use is almost certainly to rise in the next few years.

c   There's little doubt that the world population will to continue to rise for many years.

d   A scheme to help people repair their own bikes may set up if there's sufficient funding.

e   Traffic congestion in the city is expected improve after road-use charges are introduced.

Now number the sentences from 1 to 5 according to how sure the writer is that these events will happen, where 1 is the most certain and 5 is the least certain.

 ## 4 Listening: Making predictions

Listen to two friends, Laura and Martin, discussing the future and circle the letter of the correct option to complete each sentence.

1   Laura is _____ that she'll go to university.

    A   absolutely certain

    B   fairly sure

    C   unsure

2   Martin is _____ about what will happen to the world's forests.

    A   more certain than Laura

    B   as certain as Laura

    C   less sure than Laura

3   Laura will _____ do some voluntary work for an environmental charity.

    A   almost definitely

    B   probably

    C   probably not

4 Martin is most likely to do a sponsored _____ to raise money for charity.

  A swim

  B walk

  C silence

5 Laura thinks current global temperatures _____ 2°C.

  A will rise less than

  B will rise by about

> Unit 5
Entertainment

A Cinema and other forms of entertainment

1 Film vocabulary

Circle or underline the correct word from each pair in *italics*.

CB Section A2

a Who designed the *dress / costumes* for the screen adaptation of *Macbeth*?

b I prefer to check the *reviews / assessments* of a film before deciding whether to see it.

c A famous Hollywood actress has the starring role, while less well-known actors and actresses make up the rest of the *cast / group*.

d There were so many different *figures / characters* in the film, I found it very confusing.

e If the first *scene / section* in a film doesn't grab his attention, he quickly loses interest.

f Comedy, tragedy and romance are examples of different *styles / genres*.

g The film was so popular that the queue for tickets at the *box office / movie desk* reached the corner of the street.

2 More film vocabulary

Add the missing letters to the incomplete words in these sentences.

CB Section A2

a The thriller we went to see had many sp _ _ _ _ _ _ e _ _ _ _ _ _ s, including a very realistic earthquake

b The best actors and actresses of the year receive O _ _ _ _ s in a prize-giving ceremony in Hollywood.

c The film had many exotic s _ _ _ _ s, including a luxury cruise ship, a desert island and an Arabian palace.

d In the school play, all the children, even the youngest, were given a r _ _ e to play.

e The film kept me in terrible s _ _ _ _ _ se because I wasn't sure if the heroine would be rescued before the ship sank.

f The cartoon did not have an important m _ _ _ _ ge about the meaning of life, but it made the children laugh a lot.

64

Unit 5: Entertainment

g   I think Leonardo DiCaprio is a powerful actor but I found his
    p _ _ _ _ _ _ _ nce in his latest film rather disappointing.

h   She is quite a good actress but I don't think she will ever be a real
    s _ _ _ _ r.

3 So . . . that and such . . . that

CB Section A7

Add an adjective or an adjective + noun to complete these sentences. Don't use *nice* or *good*!

a   It was such a(n) _____ _____ that she won the Oscar for Best Actress.

b   It was such a(n) _____ _____ that I had to read on to the end.

c   I thought he was such a(n) _____ _____, I can't wait to see his next film.

d   Jack is so _____ in the role of romantic hero that I almost fell in love with him.

e   The tragic ending was so _____, I felt exhausted by the end.

f   There was such a _____ queue for tickets that I gave up and went home.

g   The soundtrack was so _____ that Demis went straight onto the website and downloaded it.

h   The final scene is so _____, you should be prepared for tears.

B Describing and recommending films

1 Odd word out

CB Section B2

Cross out the adjective that does not sound right in these sentences.

a   In my opinion, this film shouldn't be missed – it's really *impressive / magnificent / superb / memorable / conscious / enjoyable / wonderful*.

b   This is one of the most *engaging / disturbing / powerful / sufficient / delightful / remarkable / thrilling* dramas I've seen in years.

c   The costumes in the movie looked absolutely *stunning / substantial / tremendous / beautiful / unbelievable / incredible / astonishing*.

2 Collocations

Decide which of the nouns in the box can follow the adjectives.
Sometimes more than one noun is possible.

CB Section B3

| animation | horror film | documentary | comedy | crime film |
| thriller |

stylish _____   terrifying _____

atmospheric _____   thought-provoking _____

witty _____   skilful _____

3 Describing films

Complete sentences a–h using endings 1–8. Write the number in the box next to the correct starter phrase.

CB Sections B4 and B5

a   Mesmerising special effects and a gripping plot make this latest *Star Wars* movie ☐

b   The tense opening scene had us all ☐

c   If you like witty dialogue and hilarious situations, ☐

d   We thought the quirky cartoon characters ☐

e   During the poignant final scene, ☐

f   When the gangsters are finally captured by the police, ☐

g   Although the plot was rather slow-moving and predictable, ☐

h   The costumes and dazzling settings of this historical romance ☐

1   this enjoyable comedy will be just right for you.

2   were both original and engaging.

3   will transport you back to the beauty of an earlier age.

4   you won't be able to hold back the tears.

Unit 5: Entertainment

5 essential for science-fiction fans everywhere.

6 the skilful performances more than made up for it.

7 on the edge of our seats.

8 we all breathed a sigh of relief.

4 Describing plots

CB Section B5

In reviews, the action of a film is typically described in the present tense. Read these plot descriptions and correct any mistakes in the verb tenses. There are two mistakes in each text.

a   After her mother dies in a tragic accident, Anja has decided to change her life. She starts a job in a new city and met Max, a taxi driver with a difference.

b   An earthquake, a mudslide and an aeroplane crash . . . this latest James Bond movie has the most mesmerising special effects yet. Bond had investigated a CIA agent and a fantastic speedboat chase follows. Forced to defend himself any way he can, everything became a weapon – even sharks!

c   Harold leaves his dull job in Mexico City to begun a new career in Costa Rica with his son, Danny, a bad-tempered teenager. Relations between father and son deteriorate until Dad needs the money for a life-saving operation. It's all up to Danny – but can he done it?

d   Julia Inara portrays Lucia, a chef with no common sense. Lucia inherits her aunt's restaurant, then nearly ruined it. Enter gentle bank clerk Tony, who is detecting the real problems behind the business.

e   Victor is a rich city trader, only interested in enjoying himself. Life is changing when he travels to the countryside to take over his grandfather's farm. Victor hates rural life, but when farmgirl Zoe has fallen in love with him, he suddenly has a choice to make.

f   Tony loses his four-year-old daughter Kerry in a crowded supermarket. Despite desperate police searches, Kerry is never found. Ten years later, a girl knocked on the door. Could this be Kerry? And if so, why did she have no memory of her family?

g   The crew of a submarine are almost at the bottom of the ocean when the engine room caught fire. Can superhero Jose reach them in time? There is no margin for error in this thrilling film!

Now answer these questions. There may be more than one answer for each question.

In which review(s):

a   does someone move to a different home?   _____

b   is there an unexpected visitor?   _____

c   can you find the name of a dangerous creature?   _____

d   does someone try to help someone else or other people?   _____

e   is there mention of people's job titles?   _____

f   do people fall in love?   _____

5 Pre-listening task

Use the words and phrases in the box to complete the sentences.
Use a dictionary if necessary. You may need to change the form of some of the words.

> milestone   endearing   in earnest   make a name for yourself
> breakthrough   lap up   two-dimensional   take shape

a   The film slowly began to _____ and the director was pleased with the results.

b   Henrietta became well-known after _____ by working on several successful films.

c   The audience loved the animation and _____ the amusing, original script too.

d   Nothing like it had ever been made before – it was a true

_____ in the history of cinema.

e   Although some writing had been done, work on the script only began

_____ when several new writers were employed.

f   The animation looked very _____, as though the characters and settings were just drawings on a page.

g   The characters are so _____ that you end up wanting to take them home with you!

h   Animating movies using only computers was a real

_____ in how films are made.

Unit 5: Entertainment

 6 Listening for gist and detail

Listen to a film lecturer giving a talk about the making of a children's film called *Toy Story*, which was the first full-length movie made using only CGI (computer-generated imagery). Circle the letter of the correct answer to complete the sentences.

CB Sections B8 and B9

1 The first film to use CGI was made in _____.

   A 1973   B 1976   C 1982

2 Production company Pixar's first job was to create the _____ required for the film.

   A story   B characters   C technology

3 In the first version of the story, the main character was too _____, so this was changed.

   A pessimistic   B aggressive   C dull

4 Some people felt that an early version of the script did not have enough _____, so some were added.

   A unfunny jokes B dull storylines C human characters

5 A total of _____ people created the computer animation for the film.

   A 27   B 80   C 356

6 Pixar was unhappy with the _____ of the final film.

   A length   B picture quality C soundtrack

7 Pixar would probably describe the making of *Toy Story* as _____.

   A relatively easy, due to the help they got from other individuals and companies

   B reasonably difficult, but made easier by CGI not being a new technology

   C a tough challenge, with problems to overcome at every stage of production

8 From this talk, we learn that *Toy Story*'s success was _____.

   A critical to the survival of Pixar

   B guaranteed due to the film being highly original

   C partly due to Pixar's good reputation with the public

7 Word formation: Adjectives and evaluative adverbs

CB Sections B2 and B10

Use the correct form of the words in the box to complete the film review.

> grip   personal   fortunate   like   entertain   mystery   please
> incident   expect   thank   power   frank

Review of *The Last Chance*

I must admit that my **(a)** _____ were not very high when I sat down on the front row to watch *The Last Chance*. Although many cinemagoers disagreed, I'd **(b)** _____ found much of director Craig Halstead's previous work dull and far from **(c)** _____. So what a **(d)** _____ surprise *The Last Chance* turned out to be! The main character, Ramona, is a hugely **(e)** _____ young mother, who struggles to look after her two young children while attempting to discover what has happened to her husband, who has **(f)** _____ disappeared. The actor who plays Ramona, Sheena Collins, (who has, **(g)** _____, appeared in all four of Halstead's films to date) puts in a **(h)** _____ performance, and the plot is **(i)** _____, keeping me on the edge of my seat throughout the film's 97 minutes. **(j)** _____, however, the movie's soundtrack lets the film down. It is, quite **(k)** _____, awful but this is, **(l)** _____, the only weak point in this otherwise wonderful movie.

8 Comprehension

Circle the letter of the correct answer to these these questions about the film review in Activity 7.

1. How did the reviewer feel before watching *The Last Chance*?
    A eager to see a film that was popular with others
    B fairly sure that it would be disappointing
    C interested to see the work of a new director

2 What does the reviewer say about the lead actor?

   A She was better in other films they have seen.

   B The role she plays is too challenging for her.

   C The reviewer was impressed by her abilities.

3 What disappointed the reviewer about the film?

   A the music

   B the plot

   C the length

C Reading and television

1 Choose the best word

Complete each sentence by circling the letter of the best word or phrase.

1 I prefer an intriguing plot, rather than a _____ one where I can guess the ending.

   A predictable   B dramatic   C secure   D gripping

2 The road safety campaign on TV used _____ to frighten children into taking the dangers of roads and traffic more seriously.

   A painful stories   B shock tactics   C medical care   D expert information

3 Many parents read to young children in order to _____ them mentally.

   A increase   B grow   C spread   D stimulate

4 Marianna enjoys _____ pursuits like writing poetry, making clothes and playing the guitar.

   A creative   B imaginary   C intellectual   D physical

5 As well as the text, the book contains beautiful _____ of some of the scenes and characters, drawn by the author herself.

   A visuals   B graphics   C illustrations   D diagrams

2 Text completion

Complete this text about the future of reading by putting one word in each space.

Many people claim that the 21st century will see the end of buying novels and reading **(a)** _____ pleasure. They say that reading **(b)** _____ dull and old-fashioned compared **(c)** _____ other kinds **(d)** _____ more sophisticated entertainment. Modern technology, as we know, is constantly making amusements such **(e)** _____ computer games more and more stimulating. **(f)** _____, the development of the internet means that even **(g)** _____ you do want to read novels, you can do so electronically **(h)** _____ e-books. Consequently, there will be no need to have even **(i)** _____ single book in your house. It's hard **(j)** _____ believe, however, that everyone will want to give **(k)** _____ the pleasure of browsing through a cosy bookshop on a rainy afternoon. **(l)** _____ you want some relaxing holiday reading, it's easier to **(m)** _____ a paperback to the beach, where you won't have to worry about getting sand in an e-book reader. Books make ideal presents, too, and are much more exciting to unwrap **(n)** _____ receiving a book in digital format.

3 Sentence correction

Insert the missing word in the right place in each of these sentences.

a   Our visit to town to buy the latest 'Glass House' novel was a waste time as all the shops had sold out.

b   My cousin's school marks for literature are always better mine.

c   The novel is about a young boy growing in a poor family in South America.

d   Some people say children have no right decide what they read, but I don't agree.

e   Our class is going to have discussion about the pros and cons of television.

f   His eye injury meant that he was able to read for a few days.

g   The book is about Chen, who was brought by his aunt after his parents died.

h   This book is not as modern the last one I read.

4 Understanding pie charts

Study the pie chart, produced by a public library, which shows the kinds of books borrowed over a 12-month period. Decide if the six statements are true (✓) or false (✗).

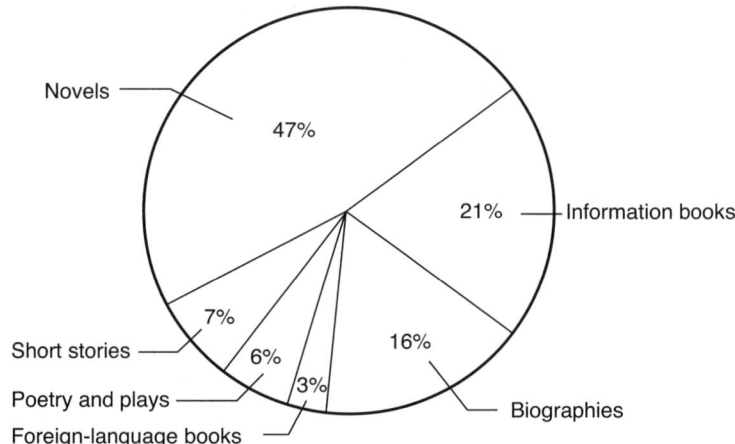

a   Information books were the most popular kind of book borrowed from the library.   _____

b   More collections of short stories were borrowed than books of poetry and plays.   _____

c Fewer biographies were borrowed than information books.

d Three times as many information books were borrowed as books of short stories.

e Books in foreign languages were the least popular.

f Over half of all books borrowed were novels.

Now write two more true sentences of your own using the information from the pie chart.

....

....

D Writing a book review

1 Developing your writing style

CB Section D4

Extracts a–h are from students' film and book reviews. Match them with comments 1–8, written in a more complex style. Write the letter next to the correct extract.

a *I think this story that I got from the library is the one that I like the most because it is a good story and more exciting than other stories I have read.*

b *I liked the things about life years and years ago in history times because it is not how life is now in modern days, but the people in this book are not like real people.*

c *I think this film made me laugh a lot at the funny things the people in it do, and I definitely think there are some things you will laugh a lot at when you see it too.*

d *You go to a lot of nice places in the world in this film, like a beach. But in my own real opinion, the film's story is not one that you can believe is true like other films.*

e *I really think the lady who wrote this book, whose name I forget, really did her best at writing it.*

f *The only person you will like in this book is a young guy who has a new job which he gets because he wants to be a policeman as a career. He is a nice person and you will like him very much, but he always believes things that even those bad guys in the book are telling him.*

g *You want to read on more and more with this book because you want to know what is going to happen to the people in it, but at the same time you think it might be bad, but you cannot guess what is going to happen to them even when you are reading it.* ☐

h *When I read the book, the main gentleman in the book is 18 at the beginning of the book and he is 19 at the end of the book. And when I went to see the film about the book, the gentleman in it looked about 30 or 31 years of age. That was much too old than he should have been to be really like he was in the book.* ☐

1 It's the most gripping story I have ever read.
2 In the screen adaptation of the novel, the hero looks too old for the part.
3 Although the locations are exotic, the plot is ridiculous.
4 The author's technical skill is superb.
5 The suspense is great.
6 The hero is a likeable but naive trainee police cop.
7 The comic scenes are so hilarious you'll have trouble holding on to your popcorn.
8 Although I enjoyed the 19th-century setting, the characters were not really convincing.

2 Language round-up

Decide whether the following sentences make sense. Give them either a tick (✓) or a (✗).

CB Section D5

a You'll be excited by the slow and predictable plot. _____

b A crime writer has to be incredibly careful when developing the plot. _____

c Jason decided to make his own way in life by becoming a writer like his father. _____

d There wasn't enough room for everyone to sit down in the spacious dining room. _____

e We have very witty new furniture at home. _____

f The hero, Vicki, enjoyed being the target of constant harassment from other students. _____

g The 'Secret of the Sword' series was made on location at the local film studio. _____

h In the book, the injured mountaineer survived for 10 days before he was rescued. _____

i   The hero's rebellious attitude made her very unpopular with the teachers at school.   _____

j   His overconfident image made him the perfect choice to portray the compassionate doctor in the film.   _____

3 Writing a book review

Write a review of a non-fiction book you have read about real-life events or people, such as a biography or autobiography of a famous person or a book about a historical period or event. In your review:

> CB Sections D8, D9 and D10

- include an effective first paragraph that involves the reader and makes them want to read more
- explain what or who the book is about
- give details of some of the content of the book
- give your opinions on how well you think the book is written
- say who you think would enjoy reading the book.

Unit 5: Entertainment

4 Using the present perfect to talk about experiences

CB Grammar spotlight

Remember that we use the present perfect to talk about experiences we have or haven't had throughout our whole lives or since a specific time in the past:

I <u>have been</u> to South America four times. *(in my whole life)*

I <u>have never seen</u> a Star Wars film. *(in my whole life)*

Helmut <u>has lost</u> seven kilograms since he started his diet. *(since starting the diet)*

Correct the mistakes in the sentences. There are two mistakes in each.

a   Emil has started directing films when he was 18 years old, so he developed a lot of experience since then.

b   It's one of the most thrilling books she ever reads, so I have finished it very quickly.

c   Laura doesn't go to the cinema very much recently, but she has gone a lot when she was younger.

d   The kind of programmes on television changed a lot since the 1950s, and there has been much less variety available back then.

e   I don't know how many times I saw this film, but it must be about five times since it has first come out.

> Unit 6
Travel and the outdoor life

A Holiday time

1 Vocabulary check

Fill in each gap with a suitable word or phrase from the box.
Be careful – there are two more than you need!

> CB Section A1

| culture and customs | nightlife | holiday resorts | tourism | scenery |
| travel websites | fully equipped campsite | fun activities |

a It can be hard staying in a tent if it rains, so we felt lucky to be staying on a

_____, which had hot showers, washing machines and a shop.

b We looked at the holidays on lots of _____ before choosing to go to Cyprus last summer.

c The country we visited was so different from our own that, at first, we couldn't understand the way of life. Gradually, however, we got to know the

people and came to appreciate their _____.

d The town we live in is also a popular _____ , with a lovely beach and many places of entertainment for tourists.

e Amalia's village is very peaceful, with no clubs or any other kind of

_____.

f Our area is rather flat and uninteresting, so we usually want to see

mountains, lakes and other kinds of interesting _____ on holiday.

2 Pre-reading task

Circle the letter of the best option to complete each sentence. Use a dictionary if you need to.

1. If you use a _____, you can breathe with your face underwater while you're swimming at the surface.

    A mask B snorkel C reef

2. I love the _____ of the countryside here – it's so calm and there's no noise at all.

    A tranquility B capacity C softness

3. You could see the island from the coast – it wasn't far at all from the_____ .

    A homeland B inland C mainland

4. The _____ of the town where we stayed were all very friendly to tourists.

    A populations B neighbourhoods C residents

5. The hot water appears naturally out of the ground – it's a hot _____.

    A spring B well C tap

6. I practise _____ every morning because it makes me feel calm and relaxed.

    A reduction B meditation C location

3 Five-minute reading task: Scanning

Read the three short texts about day trips from popular holiday resorts then answer the questions that follow. Try to complete the task in five minutes or less.

> CB Sections A4 and A5

> **1 The Blue Hole, Dahab, Egypt**
>
> The famous Blue Hole is a 100-metre-deep hole in the coral reef near Dahab. We offer day trips there for just $75 per person, with reductions for groups of six or more. After a two-hour drive from the popular resort of Sharm-el-Sheikh, you'll arrive in Dahab just in time for lunch at one of the many local cafés (not included, but costs around $7 per person). After lunch, you'll be taken to the Blue Hole, just 7 km from Dahab, and you'll spend the afternoon snorkelling, swimming and relaxing there. Bring your own face mask and snorkel so that you can see the thousands of colourful reef fish. We'll stop for an hour in the desert before returning to Sharm-el-Sheikh, so you can experience the peace and tranquility of this beautiful location as day turns to night.

> **2 Nimara Cave, Marmaris, Turkey**
>
> Nimara Cave is located on Heaven Island, near Marmaris. Confusingly, Heaven Island isn't really an island: it's connected to the mainland by a thin strip of land, which we'll walk across to reach the cave. According to recent research, human presence in the cave dates back to almost 12 000 years ago. It's found at the highest point of Heaven Island and was used mainly as a place of worship by the ancient residents of the town of Nimara, now known as Marmaris. The cave is a protected area, and you're sure to see the rare species of butterfly that it's famous for, as well as many other interesting creatures. A bargain at just $80!
>
> **3 Jungle Tour, Krabi, Thailand**
>
> This $100 tour is limited to eight people, so you'll get to know the other visitors and your guide well during the day. Setting off from Krabi Town by minibus, visitors are taken first to the hot spring waterfall. You can bathe in the warm water of the various pools that make up the waterfall before taking a swim in the beautiful Emerald Pool nearby. After a walk in the rainforest along the jungle nature trail, your tour fee also includes a delicious Thai lunch at a local restaurant. The tour continues to Tiger Cave Temple to visit the meditation centre there, returning to Krabi well before it gets dark.

Which tour:

a includes seeing some uncommon species of insect? ☐

b will always be with only a few people? ☐

c is the cheapest? ☐

d offers a meal that is included in the price? ☐

e is cheaper if you go in a large group? ☐

f leaves from a place that has changed its name? ☐

g says what type of vehicle tourists will travel in? ☐

h mentions something that tourists should take with them? ☐

4 Paragraphing and punctuation

Add the punctuation and paragraphing to this article about the persuasive techniques that holiday company websites use to encourage people to book with them. Remember – read the text through first to get the gist. Write the corrected version below.

CB Sections A4 and A5

> recently our class looked at a website advertising an activity holiday we identified the persuasive techniques advertisers use to convince potential customers to choose this kind of holiday firstly we looked at the photographs showing young people doing interesting activities the activities looked very appealing and succeeded in the advertisers aim of making us want to find out more about the holidays the target group for this kind of holiday is teenagers and we noticed how in order to increase a sense of identification young people of similar ages and backgrounds to ourselves were chosen for the pictures we also studied the information given on the website this was also persuasive as comments such as every minute of the day is filled with fun were used to look like real facts rather than just the advertisers opinions I think by choosing scenic locations happy-looking people and exciting activities the holiday company achieved their aim of making the holiday seem attractive in addition they cleverly disguised any negative aspects of the holiday if you are thinking of booking on a holiday website remember the advertiser wants you to buy the holiday and will only show its good points so think of its potential drawbacks for yourself before making your mind up

5 Language study: Using modifiers before adjectives

CB Section A8

Underline or circle the correct modifier in these sentences.

a It was a *fairly / very* windy day, so there was a bit of wind but not too much.

b His new bike cost thousands of dollars, so it was *quite / extremely* expensive.

c We left our phones and money in very strong lockers, so they were *a little / quite* safe.

d The path was only *slightly / really* uphill, so it wasn't a very difficult walk.

B Outdoor activities

1 Text completion

CB Section B2

This report, about the advantages and disadvantages of swimming, appeared on a holiday website for teenagers. Fill in the gaps by reading for meaning and choosing from the vocabulary. There is one extra word in the box.

> life-saving   sensitive   risky   supervised   shallow   warnings
> sea   emergency   costume   flexibility   trunks   exercise   strain

Next to football and cycling, swimming is one of the most popular activities.

It develops stamina, **(a)** _____ and strength. It's good for people at all

Unit 6: Travel and the outdoor life

levels of fitness, as it doesn't place any **(b)** _____ on the joints. It's simple to arrange, it's not expensive and the only equipment you need is a(n) **(c)** _____ or a pair of swimming **(d)** _____.

The best places for swimming are **(e)** _____ public pools, although the high levels of chlorine used can be unpleasant. If your eyes are **(f)** _____ to chlorine, wearing goggles is recommended. Swimming in lakes, rivers or the sea can be thrilling but is also **(g)** _____. You should always obey red flag **(h)** _____ and be aware of tides and currents that can drag you out to **(i)** _____. Never dive in **(j)** _____ water, as this can lead to serious injury.

As your swimming skills increase, you can think about taking **(k)** _____ certificates which will prepare you for any **(l)** _____ in water.

2 Developing your writing style

Read this student's description of hiking. Circle or underline the correct word or phrase from each pair in *italics*.

CB Section B3

I love *being / to be* in the fresh air, and I have belonged to a hiking club *from / since* I was 14. I particularly enjoy *exploring / to explore* little-known areas of countryside *where / which* nature still seems to be *definitely / completely* wild and untouched. I've learnt a lot about wildlife and have succeeded in *identifying / to identify* many rare birds and delicate wild flowers. I usually take a camera so that I can *capture / to capture* these moments, and I get great pleasure *from looking / to look* at the pictures afterwards. Spotting a fox coming out of its den is *a / one* particular thrill. Walking home in the evenings when the stars look *like / as though* jewels in the night sky is wonderful too. Hiking is great for people *they / who* need a relaxing but also *bodily / physically* challenging outdoor activity *it / which* provides exercise without pressure or competition.

3 Pre-listening task

You are going to listen to a college student called Anna, who has just finished working as a volunteer at a summer camp, organising and supervising activities for teenagers. Write a paragraph explaining why you would or would not like to work as a volunteer at a summer camp.

CB Section B7

....

....

....

....

....

....

4 Listening for gist

Listen to Anna describing her experience of volunteering at the summer camp, then answer these questions.

CB Section B8

a How much do you think Anna enjoyed working at the summer camp?

....

....

b What did Anna find particularly difficult about volunteering at the summer camp? List three things.

....

....

....

5 Listening for detail

Listen to the audio again, and fill in the gaps in these sentences.

CB Section B9

a Anna worked as a volunteer for _____ weeks at the summer camp.

b Anna enjoyed learning _____ at the camp, which she'd never tried before.

Unit 6: Travel and the outdoor life

c   Anna hated cleaning the _____ at the summer camp.

d   Anna found _____ the most difficult thing to do when entertaining the teenagers.

e   Anna will fly home from the _____ of Canada.

6 Blame and responsibility

Use a word from the box to complete the sentences.

CB Section B11

| should   responsibility   fault   things   down   responsible |
| blame   guilty |

a   You shouldn't _____ yourself for the children not enjoying the holiday – it was because the weather was bad, so it's not your _____.

b   Making sure we've got the passports is your _____, so it's totally _____ to you that we forgot them.

c   Haider feels very _____ about getting lost and missing the plane. He _____ have checked the map more carefully.

d   You're not _____ for the car breaking down – it's just one of those _____.

7 Colloquial expressions: 'Body' idioms

Complete each sentence with an idiomatic expression from the box. There is one more than you need. The first one has been done as an example.

CB Sections B14 and B15

| ~~bite my tongue~~   behind my back   blew my mind   a straight face |
| off my chest   give me a hand   heart of gold |

a   When my dad asked me what I thought about his new trousers, I had to _bite my tongue_. I thought they were awful, but I couldn't tell him that! I said they suited him.

85

b I couldn't believe it when I heard my best friend had been saying horrible things about me _____.

c Going to New York for the first time _____. I can't think of a more exciting city.

d I had to ask Jonas to _____ with installing the new software – I had no idea what I was doing!

e I write down all my worries in a diary. I find it is a good way to get problems _____.

f When Mrs Sohail saw her little boy dressed up in a funny costume for the nursery school play, she tried to look serious, but it was hard to keep _____.

8 Word building: Adjective suffixes

CB Section B16

Fill the gaps with adjectives formed from the nouns in brackets. Add *-able*, *-ic* or *-ous*. Remember that adding a suffix can mean spelling changes, too.

a The most _____ part of our trip was the visit to the Roman ruins. (*memory*)

b Not all snakes are _____, you know. Some are completely harmless. (*poison*)

c The island's _____ scenery and great weather made up for the rather _____ accommodation. (*drama, base*)

d The weather on Cephalonia can be _____ in the autumn. (*change*)

e The rescuers were awarded medals for their _____ act. (*courage*)

f We rented a wonderfully _____ apartment with a fantastic view of the bay. (*space*)

C Tourism: The pros and cons

1 Text completion

Read this article about eco-tourism. Circle or underline the correct word or phrase from each pair in *italics*.

CB Section C2

Eco-tourism is a fast-growing form of tourism that *arranges / gives* trips to little-known regions of the world such as the Namib desert or the Malaysian rainforest.

According to / Regarding eco-tourist organisations, their approach avoids many of the drawbacks associated *to / with* ordinary tourism. Eco-tourists *observe / recognise* birds and animal behaviour, *study / learn* plant life, use canoes in preference *of / to* motorboats, live with local inhabitants rather than in hotels and *do / make* everything possible not to *interfere / disturb* the natural environment.

However, the opponents of eco-tourism *disagree / argue* that it is no better than conventional tourism. They say that in areas *when / where* the ecosystem is not stable, the effect of large numbers of tourists *to / on* these environments is *even / further* more devastating.

2 Building an email from prompts

Esther recently visited the Italian islands of Sicily and Sardinia. Create a complete email about her trip using these prompts.

CB Section C7

Subject:

Hi Wayan,

Just quick email / tell you about / our wonderful holiday / visiting / beautiful islands / Sicily and Sardinia. They be places / I never go to / but always want / visit. Sicily have / grand but stormy past. We see / traces Arabic and Greek influences / in buildings / ruined temples / we visit. We spend two nights / capital Palermo / which be full of / life. We also hire bicycles / and cycle / sleepy villages. We be / impressed / gentle pace / life / warmth / people.

Highlight / trip / be picnic / magical mountain setting. We sit / near stream. Far below / we can see / Mediterranean / gleam / in sunshine. Only sound / be rustling / wind / trees.

It be / holiday / I never forget!

Write soon!

Love,

Esther

....
....
....
....
....
....
....
....
....
....

3 Understanding maps

Look carefully at the map showing Sicily and Sardinia, then answer the questions.

a What are the names of the principal towns in Sicily?

....

....

b Which city is further north, Cagliari or Naples?

....

c Which island is further west, Sicily or Sardinia?

....

d Which mountain is shown on the map, and how high is it?

....

e Naples is about 100 kilometres from Rome – true or false?

....

4 Language study: Adverbs as modifiers

Complete each sentence with a suitable phrase from the box.
There is one more than you need.

CB Section C9

> hardly recognisable   frantically busy   dazzlingly bright
> exceptionally interesting   bitterly cold   badly designed
> incredibly painful   completely exhausted   mentally tiring

a Before I went to the dentist, my bad tooth was _____.

b I have always liked Anita Desai's novels – the last one I read was

_____.

c I was _____ last weekend trying to finish all my geography and biology coursework.

d The midday sun shining on the sea was _____.

e Meg lost so much weight during her illness that she was

_____.

f The children put on warm coats, hats and scarves before going out, as the

weather had turned _____.

g After a long day hiking and climbing, they were all

_____.

h Jordi's work as a computer programmer is not physically demanding, but it is

_____.

5 Developing your writing style

Rewrite this description of a holiday destination, Paradise Island, to make it more interesting. Try to improve its style.

CB Section C13

> Paradise Island is shaped like a diamond. It has a lot of rocks on the coastline. The sea is clean. You can see fish in the sea. The beach is white. There are many shells on the beach. There are palm trees along the beach. There are many flowers. You can smell the flowers in the air. There are many birds. The birds sing a lot. The sunsets are good. The sky looks pink. At night there are many stars. There are no tower blocks. There is no traffic. There are no crowds. It is peaceful.

Unit 6: Travel and the outdoor life

D Personal challenges

1 Reading an example email

CB Section D1

The adjective and infinitive construction is often used to express opinion. For example:

It is *hard to find* a better-quality resort.

It is *easy to forget* that Sicily was once the most fought-over island in the Mediterranean.

Choose the best phrase to fill each gap in this email to a friend. There is one more phrase than you need.

> awful to live in   pleasing to look at   difficult to know
> hard to believe   expensive to heat   marvellous to visit
> idealistic of me to think   easy to maintain

Hi Tamara

How are you doing?

I'm so jealous that you've actually been to Egypt and have seen some of the most famous sights there. I've always been fascinated by Egypt because it's such a truly astonishing country! Did you know that the ancient Egyptians are said to have been the world's first architects? It's **(a)** _____ that they were able to build the pyramids without modern equipment and technology. It would be **(b)** _____ Egypt like you, and see for myself the way they were built.

My dream for the future is to design buildings. So many modern homes are **(c)** _____ because they're badly designed and constructed, and require constant repairs. They often have poorly fitting doors and windows, which makes them **(d)** _____ in cold weather. Maybe it's **(e)** _____ that I could design the perfect home, but if I became an architect, I'd like to design practical buildings that are **(f)** _____ and, because I think beauty is important, **(g)** _____ as well.

Anyway, write and tell me about your hopes and ambitions for the future.

Samuel

SUCCESS INTERNATIONAL ENGLISH SKILLS FOR CAMBRIDGE IGCSE™: WORKBOOK

Now write four sentences of your own, choosing from the following phrases.

> exciting to watch   impossible to describe   hard to accept
> difficult to cope with   lucky to win   nice to talk   kind of you to take
> delighted to hear

....

....

....

....

Look again at the first paragraph of the email. There are five sentences, each with its own function. Write the number of the sentence next to its function.

A   A rhetorical question that provides a link to the writer's own ambition.   ☐

B   A summary of the paragraph, which also provides a connection with the reader.   ☐

C   A reference to information provided by the reader in their previous email.   ☐

D   An expression of a personal ambition.   ☐

E   A link between information provided previously by the reader and the writer's interests.   ☐

2 Compound nouns with *snow* and *sun*

CB Section D4

Complete the compound nouns by writing either *snow* or *sun* in each space.

_____shine   _____roof   _____drift

_____burn   _____screen   _____board

_____storm   _____flake   _____tan

_____light   _____stroke

_____hat   _____plough

_____ball   _____bathe

Unit 6: Travel and the outdoor life

3 Spelling revision

CB Section D5

Make adjectives by adding -y to the words in brackets to fill the gaps. Remember to make any other necessary spelling changes.

a Oppressive, _____ weather is more common in the summer. (*thunder*)

b _____, polluted air blocked out the sunlight. (*smoke*)

c When the sun shines through a thin, _____ cloud, a coloured ring like a halo may appear. (*ice*)

d It was too _____ and _____ to even think of going for a walk. (*wind, rain*)

4 Building a text from notes

CB Section D8

Turn these notes about a camping holiday into complete sentences by adding any necessary words, such as verbs, linking words or articles. The first one has been done as an example.

a arrived campsite – plan to stay few days

We arrived at the campsite where we plan to stay for a few days.

b fishing in nearby lake – didn't catch anything

....

c caught in thunderstorm – no coats – soaked to skin

....

d to country market – bought brand new DVD dirt cheap

....

e terrific walk through pine-scented forest – picnic near waterfall

....

f met man in forest – lent us binoculars to look at deer

....

g whole hour watching breathtaking sunset – sky completely dark

....

5 Adverbs of frequency

Put these adverbs of frequency into the correct order, with most frequent at the top and least frequent at the bottom.

> never   usually   sometimes   always   seldom   hardly ever
> often   rarely

CB Grammar spotlight

Most frequent   _____

_____

_____

_____

_____

_____

_____

Least frequent   _____

Rewrite the sentences with an appropriate adverb of frequency in the correct place. In some sentences, more than one answer is possible.

a   I go to the cinema – maybe just once or twice a year.

....

b   Kendra doesn't go to Italy on holiday – she goes to other countries from time to time.

....

c   Marek likes going on day trips when he's on holiday, but most of the time, he stays at the beach.

....

d   Maria eats out when she's on holiday, but occasionally she cooks something at her rented apartment.

....

e   Hector is late when he has to catch a plane – he arrives early every time!

....

Unit 7
Student life

A Challenges of student life

1 Challenges of student life

What are these students talking about? Match each comment with the correct explanation. There are two more than you need.

> CB Section A1

a   Can you believe it? My new red shirt has run. Everything is bright pink – even my football shorts!

b   The money was paid into my account yesterday so I now have enough to live on.

c   He said the spots on my leg hadn't got better because I was taking the wrong medicine.

d   I phone every Sunday evening to let them know how I'm getting on.

e   I can't go on the picnic. The deadline for my history assignment is Monday, so I'm working all Sunday. Everyone will be out so I'll get a bit of peace and quiet.

f   The rent's not too bad but I've got bills and bus fares on top of that. I have to be careful not to spend money on things I don't need.

g   It gets really hot, so I have to be careful not to burn holes in my shirts.

h   I hate tinned stuff, so I pop down to the market at the end of the day. You can get fresh fruit and vegetables cheaper then.

1   a bank transfer
2   ironing clothes
3   eating well
4   organising time and working alone
5   managing on a budget
6   the laundry
7   a medical problem
8   keeping in touch with the family

2 Conversation study

CB Section A4

Tick (✓) the best response to each of the following comments in a friendly conversation between friends.

1 I couldn't find a pair of socks that would match this morning. I'm wearing two odd ones under these trousers!

   A   You must have been out of your mind with worry. _____

   B   At least you found an acceptable solution. _____

   C   Never mind. They don't show with those shoes. _____

   D   I can't bear to be badly dressed either. _____

2 I was painting my nails for the party when I broke one, just before I had to go out.

   A   It's a shame to see you in such a state. _____

   B   I noticed straight away they weren't right. _____

   C   You should have started again immediately. _____

   D   Oh, no! I've done that too. _____

3 I was looking after my nephew, who's only three. He was eating an apple when suddenly he started choking. He was gasping for breath but he managed to cough it up after a few seconds.

   A   You shouldn't have given him that apple. _____

   B   I expect you needed some advice about that. _____

   C   That must have been terrifying for you. _____

   D   You really need to go on a first aid course. _____

Unit 7: Student life

3 Tone and register in students' emails

CB Section A14

Read these first paragraphs of emails sent in reply to a party invitation. For each one, make notes on what is good or bad about each paragraph, then decide which opening is the most appropriate.

1

> I always need a good social life but I'm afraid I won't be coming to your party. I've been invited to a big party Barry is giving to celebrate the end of term on the same night. It's going to be fantastic, and he's taking over the whole of the University Social Centre. Maybe you should check with everyone before making plans? It's the best way of avoiding such tragic errors.

....

....

2

> Thanks so much for the invitation to your party! I wish the invitation had arrived a week earlier, because then I would have been able to come. However, last week, Barry invited me to a party he's having on the same evening and I've already said yes. I said I'd do the music for it too, so I really can't let him down now – sorry! Anyway, I hope it goes really well and that you have a great time.

....

....

3

> It was kind of you to invite me to your party. I'd really like to come but Barry's having a party too that same night and it's likely to be a bit more interesting than yours; not because of you, of course, but the music won't be as good and there won't be as many people there. Why don't you cancel it or change the date or something and come to Barry's party too? I'm sure you'd have a good time.

....

....

Most appropriate opening: _____

B The pressure of exams

1 Pre-reading task

Draw lines to match these words and phrases to their meanings.

a   constantly   highly planned, organised and structured

b   strategy   completely or very much

c   systematic   extremely important or necessary

d   effectively   refers to something that is very close to something else

e   crucial   happening all the time

f   run through   in a successful way that achieves what you want

g   thoroughly   doing something again to practise it

h   immediate   a detailed plan for achieving success

2 Reading comprehension

You are going to read how three different students prepare for important exams. Match the ideas below (a–g) with the students (1–3). There is one extra idea that you do not need to use.

CB Section B3

a   I always relax the night before an exam as it's too late to learn more. ☐

b   I do the same amount of revision each day before the exam. ☐

c   I stay up very late revising the night before each exam. ☐

d   I get people to test me on key points that I need to know. ☐

e   I make notes on all the key points as I revise them. ☐

f   I practise by doing past exam papers from previous years. ☐

g   I think about points that might be tested while I'm exercising. ☐

1 Magdalena

I'm far from being one of those people who can switch off and forget about exams when I'm not actually revising. I constantly worry about the exams and how much more work I need to do to prepare, even when I'm out on my bike. I regularly ask my parents to check I know the stuff that I'm likely to get questions on, and they're always happy to help. I never work in the evenings, especially when I've got an exam the next day. I find that information just doesn't go in at that time of day, so if there's anything I don't know by then, staying up all night isn't going to solve that problem. It's a much better strategy to watch a film, or something like that.

2 Carlos

I'm very systematic in my planning for exam study. It helps me separate revision time from relaxation time much more effectively. As I'm looking through my coursework, trying to take in the information that'll probably come up in the exam, I write down the crucial facts and figures: it seems to help me remember them. In the week running up to the test, I do six hours of this daily, split evenly between morning, afternoon and evening. That gives me time to relax and do other things like running, when I try to avoid thinking about exams or the knowledge I'll need to do well in them at all.

3 Hamida

I tend to get quite stressed out by exams, but I've found swimming helps. Somehow, doing length after length in the pool while running through what I've read earlier in the day seems to help it go in more thoroughly. Some of my classmates use exam papers that students have done over the last five or six years to help them prepare. That feels a bit like cheating to me, though. I always feel tired after each exam as I don't get much sleep in the immediate run-up to it, as I often work until three or four o'clock in the morning preparing for it. Some of my friends spend the night before taking it easy, but I can't see the sense in that at all.

3 Vocabulary: Colloquial words and phrases

CB Section B5

Which of these expressions is not associated with unhappiness from having too much to do? Tick the expression.

a stressed out

b under pressure

c snowed under

d rushed off my feet

e at a loose end

Match the halves to make complete sentences. There is one extra 'second half'.

a I was so anxious waiting my turn for the oral exam,

b I wanted to work in a restaurant in the evenings but

c You still need to have fun

d I'd been revising all day on my own in the library, so

e It's very difficult to get down to studying if

f One thing I never do after an exam is

g If I'm suffering from exam tension,

h My father has laid down the law about

1 I just had to meet my friends and have some fun.
2 even when you're under exam pressure.
3 compare answers with my friends.
4 you've lost your motivation.
5 I went out for a coffee as a way of distracting myself.
6 which was a way of using spare time constructively.
7 doing my homework before I go out in the evening.
8 I go for a long workout at the gym.
9 my parents put their foot down about it.

Unit 7: Student life

4 Language study: Giving advice

Choose the best expression to complete each piece of advice.

CB Section B7

| needs to learn   encourage   should be encouraged   needs to be seen |

a   Submitting homework on time _____ as an essential if he wants to do well.

b   Angelika _____ to ask for help in class whenever she needs it.

c   Sergio definitely _____ how to plan his revision more carefully.

d   Please _____ Asha to spend more time researching her essays.

Circle the letter of the option that shows the best way of completing these two short texts.

1   I was sorry to hear that you're finding it difficult to keep up with some of the lectures. I had the same problem at university at first because I wasn't used to having to listen and take notes at the same time. _____ trying to prepare for your lectures the night before by studying some of the subject vocabulary you might hear?

   A   It's a good idea to
   B   Have you ever thought of
   C   You really have to
   D   You could always

2   So you're not sure what topic to choose for your art project? Why not choose one you're interested in and already know something about? _____ do a project on the history of fashion. You've always been fascinated by that.

   A   How about
   B   You must
   C   You'd better
   D   You could

5 Using a more informal tone

CB Section B9

Rewrite the following sentences using the words in brackets.

a   It was wrong of you to forget Mum's birthday. She was expecting you to phone her. (*shouldn't*)

   ....

b   It isn't necessary to buy any milk when you go out. I bought two litres this morning. (*needn't*)

   ....

101

c   It's important that you take warm clothes with you. It's likely to be cold when you get to Canada. (*had better*)

   ....

d   I regret not going to bed earlier last night. (*should*)

   ....

e   It is unwise to leave your revision to the last minute. (*oughtn't*)

   ....

f   It's a pity you've already booked a taxi. I could have given you a lift home. (*needn't*)

   ....

Choose the best informal expression to complete each sentence. There is one more than you need.

> stick to   push me   make up   do my best   too much on his mind
> nag you   get on   loads

a   My friend Makeen must be the hardest-working boy in the school. He studies in the library until late every evening and does _____ at home too.

b   I can't motivate myself to study. I need someone to _____.

c   Do your parents _____ about doing homework?

d   It's no good making a work plan if you don't _____ it.

e   If I save most of the money I need for a new phone, my parents say they'll _____ the rest.

f   I tried hard in that exam because I really wanted to _____.

6 Homophones with silent letters

CB Section B10

For each of the words, find a homophone (a word that sounds the same) in the box. Write it in the space, then put brackets around the silent letter or letters. The first one has been done as an example.

Unit 7: Student life

| weigh | knight | hour | ~~heir~~ | wrote | which | scent | reign |
| | | | weight | whether | | | |

a air   _heir_   f witch   _____

b our   _____   g weather _____

c rain   _____   h way   _____

d wait   _____   i sent   _____

e night _____   j rote   _____

Choose three pairs of homophones from your list and write sentences to show their meaning.

a ....

b ....

c ....

C Studying effectively

1 Punctuation reminders: Capital letters

Some of these words need capital letters. Circle all the letters that should be capitals.

mr jones   wednesday   weekend

college   chinese   evening

assignment   september   asia

joseph   india   harvey street

CB Section C1

103

university of colorado	surgeon	bbc
castle	river nile	himalayas
baltic sea	examination	professor grivas

2 Punctuation reminders: Punctuating a text

CB Section C1

Read this extract from a school report. Rewrite it correctly, adding any necessary punctuation.

> having just marked her last revision test I am concerned that jennifers poor english is holding her back fortunately she is seeing mr barnes the language support teacher every tuesday afternoon for help with grammar spelling vocabulary and handwriting she needs to make a special effort to improve in these areas

3 Idiomatic expressions

CB Section C4

Decide whether these sentences make logical sense. Give each one a tick (✓) or a cross (✗).

a I've never broken a bone in my body, touch wood. _____

b When my friends came round, I made them welcome by giving them the cold shoulder. _____

c My classmates said the maths test was hard, but I thought it was easy – I couldn't make head nor tail of it! _____

d My brother has set his heart on becoming a professional footballer. I think he can do it. He trains really hard. _____

e My sister's Chinese course is going well. She says she feels completely out of her depth. _____

Unit 7: Student life

4 Increasing your stock of idioms

CB Section C5

Guess the meaning of the idioms in *italics*. Write your answer in the space provided.

a 'You'll have to *pull your socks up*,' said the headteacher to the student who had received low marks, 'or you'll be leaving this school without a single exam pass.'

   Meaning: _____

b Manuela was usually good at passing exams but failed two this time. She seems to be *losing her touch*.

   Meaning: _____

c Ricky hasn't told his parents he failed his exams yet, but he'll have to *face the music* at some point.

   Meaning: _____

D Advising and helping

1 Pre-listening task

Decide whether the following sentences about student life are true (✓) or false (✗). Use a dictionary to check the meaning of the words in *italics* if you need to.

a A tutorial may have a lot of students attending at the same time, but you'll only ever find a small number at a *lecture*. _____

b A *chore* is a boring kind of job you do in the house, like washing the floor. _____

c The money you *borrow* from the government to pay for your studies is called a loan. _____

d An *essay*, like a composition, is a piece of written work. _____

e Missing essay *deadlines* is not important because you can catch up later. _____

f An *assignment* is work that is usually done outside class. _____

g If you enjoy trying something new, even if you are not sure you will be successful, you like *challenges*. _____

h *Coursework* doesn't count towards the final exam marks. _____

i A *revision* timetable reminds you when your exams will take place. _____

j The marks from a *mock exam* are part of the marks given for the real exam. _____

2 Listening for gist

You will hear a university student called Jack talking to his friend Selena about some of the pressures of student life. Listen to the conversation and answer the questions.

a How happy does Jack seem with his accommodation and flatmates so far?

....

....

b How interested does Selena seem in what Jack says during the conversation? How do you know?

....

....

c What problems does Jack think might happen in his university flat in the future?

....

....

CB Section D2

3 Detailed listening

Listen to the recording again and decide whether these sentences are true (T), false (F) or not given (NG). Circle your answers.

a Jack's new flat is close to where his family lives. T / F / NG

b Six people live in Jack's flat in total. T / F / NG

c A mix of males and females are living in the flat. T / F / NG

d The flat became messy soon after the students moved in. T / F / NG

e Jack thinks he gets more chores to do than other students. T / F / NG

f The students created a plan together for doing the chores. T / F / NG

g There is usually no one in the flat during the day. T / F / NG

h Jack hasn't had much work to do at home yet. T / F / NG

CB Section D3

Unit 7: Student life

i Jack hasn't actually been to the university library yet. T / F / NG

j All the flatmates have borrowed money to study. T / F / NG

4 Email completion

Use the words in the box to form new words, then complete the extracts from emails sent to a student newspaper. The first one has been done as an example.

CB Section D7

| advise   train   ~~knock~~   appoint   embarrass   occupy   earn |

To: Alison Wu
From: Javier

In your recent article about the college counselling service, you asked readers to write in about whether or not they would see a college counsellor. Well, I definitely wouldn't!

I just don't like the idea of **(a)** _knocking_ on a stranger's door and telling them my problems. Although I visit the doctor occasionally, talking about personal problems with a counsellor would make me feel **(b)** _____. I would much rather talk to someone I know and trust, like my best friends or my parents.

Furthermore, I think counsellors could give you bad **(c)** _____. They are not like doctors or lawyers who have done a lot of **(d)** _____. As I see it, anyone can call themselves a counsellor because it is a relatively new **(e)** _____ that isn't totally regulated.

Last but not least, a counsellor may ask you to make further **(f)** _____ when you don't really need to. Perhaps I'm being cynical, but don't forget that the counsellor is **(g)** _____ money from your visits, so it's in his or her interest to continue seeing you.
Javier

Now do the same with the following email.

> discussion   choice   wonder   positively   confidence
> organisation   effective

To: Alison Wu
From: Pascale

I really enjoyed the recent article on the college counselling service – thanks! I have already made use of the service and would definitely see a counsellor again if I needed to.

Our college has (h) _____ counsellors who really understand your problems. There are actually two different ones, and you can (i) _____ which one you prefer to see. You (j) _____ your problems and are helped to discover what the best thing is to do.

I saw Mrs Hobson once when I was under a lot of exam pressure. She really helped me talk things through and (k) _____ my work better. Talking to her, I realised that my father's illness had had a bad (l) _____ on me and that my exam nerves were probably linked to that. My visits to the counsellor were completely (m) _____, so I felt secure there. Going to a college counsellor is definitely a (n) _____ move, to my mind.

Pascale

Unit 7: Student life

 5 Grammar spotlight: Modals

Modal verbs can be used in many different ways. Here are a few of them.

A Past modals

These are used to talk or write about hypothetical events in the past that did not actually happen. You form them like this:

subject + should / would / could / might / may + have + past participle

Example: I <u>could have done</u> better in my exam. (Meaning: I didn't do very well in my exam!)

B Modals with passive forms

You make passive forms with modal verbs like this:

subject + should/would/could/might/may + be + past participle

Examples:

Dictionaries <u>cannot be used</u> in the exam.

More parks <u>should be created</u> in our city.

These sentences all contain mistakes that students commonly make. Write the sentences out correctly under each one.

a The show should start at 19:30, but it actually started 45 minutes late.

   ....

b A better time could had been chosen for the concert.

   ....

c There might be made some improvements next year.

   ....

d The order must have been delivered on 23 October, but it never arrived.

   ....

e I'm glad I took that map because, without it, I was lost!

   ....

> Unit 8

The search for adventure

A The call of the sea

1 Sea vocabulary

Write the sea vocabulary words from the box next to the definitions.
What are the two extra words?

CB Section A3

| current   shore   port   seaweed   pebbles   driftwood   surf
  dunes   liner   rock |

a   Smooth, round stones   _____

b   A plant growing underwater   _____

c   Pieces of wood that float on water or are washed up
    onto the beach   _____

d   White water made by strong waves   _____

e   Water moving in one direction   _____

f   A large passenger ship   _____

g   The land along the edge of the sea   _____

h   A town with a harbour, where ships load and unload   _____

Unit 8: The search for adventure

Circle or underline the correct word from each pair in *italics*.

a   Eddie works at the *jetty / docks* unloading *cargo / baggage* from ships that transport goods from all over the world.

b   The captain stood on deck and looked carefully at the *horizon / cliffs* for signs of another ship.

c   We always check the times of high and low *tide / spray* before launching our little boat.

d   I went *snorkelling / windsurfing* on holiday and saw all kinds of fascinating sea life below the surface.

e   The *smugglers / pirates* who brought perfume and cigarettes into the country illegally have just been caught by the police.

f   Omar is hoping for the right kind of wind when he sails his *dinghy / speedboat*.

2 More sea vocabulary

CB Section A3

Add the missing letters to complete words in these sentences.

a   Sea creatures range in size from enormous w _ _ _ _ s to tiny organisms that can only be seen through a microscope.

b   A s _ _ _ _ _ r is another name for a captain.

c   There are five o _ _ _ _ s in the world – the largest is the Pacific.

d   In the past, people going on a sea v _ _ _ _ e feared fierce bands of

   p _ _ _ _ _ s who attacked ships. They stole the ship's c _ _ _ o and robbed the passengers.

e   If you see a boat in difficulty, you should immediately contact the

   c _ _ _ _ _ _ _ _ d, who will organise a rescue.

f   A l _ _ _ _ _ _ _ _ e flashes a special light out to sea to warn sailors that danger is near.

g   People say that d _ _ _ _ _ _ s are intelligent animals that can 'talk' to one another under the water.

h   My little sister loves walking along the beach, collecting sh _ _ _ s of different shapes and sizes.

i   A v _ _ _ _ l is a word that can be used for any kind of ship.

j   Sailing boats vary in type from small d _ _ _ _ _ _ s to large

   y _ _ _ _ s.

3 Reading and sequencing

CB Section A7

Match the halves to make complete sentences. Write the number of the second half next to the first half. Then put the sentences in the correct order to create a short narrative. Write the letters of the beginning of the sentence on the line below in order.

a We were beginning to despair of ever being rescued when ☐

b On this occasion, my brother and I decided ☐

c One day last summer, we went to the beach together as usual, ☐

d We didn't realise that there was a strong current ☐

e I have never been so glad ☐

f Unfortunately, there was no one else on the beach who ☐

g I live near the sea and often go to the beach ☐

h Little did we know that this decision ☐

i Before long, we were too far away from the land ☐

j We immediately started getting pulled ☐

1 would put us in real danger.
2 taking our small, inflatable boat with us.
3 with my twin brother.
4 could have seen that we were in trouble and called for help.
5 to go out much further than we usually do.
6 a fishing boat saw us and came to our rescue.
7 to call for help, even if anyone had been there.
8 to see another boat in my life!
9 further and further from the shore.
10 that flows away from the coast when you go out so far.

Correct order: _____

Unit 8: The search for adventure

4 Language study: Narrative tenses

CB Section A11

Correct the verb mistakes in these sentences. One sentence has no mistakes.

a They didn't look thin, despite the fact that they were not eating a proper meal for several weeks.

....

b At first, he has been devastated by the shipwreck, but he gradually got used to his situation.

....

c When we arrived at the harbour, the ferry we going to catch had already left.

....

d Irene had been feeling sick on the boat, so she felt relieved when the boat finally docked.

....

e The crew managed to escape from the ship before it has sunk.

....

f I was looking on the floor of the café for a ring I had misplaced, when the owner came up and ask if I lost anything.

....

g I was skateboarding in the park when I fallen over and hurt my knee badly.

....

5 Text completion

Read this story about a seaside holiday. Fill the gaps by adapting the words in brackets.

A happy ending

Have you ever _____ (be) on holiday with your family and really wished

you had a friend of your own age around? Last summer, my parents and I were

113

_____ (stay) in a caravan on the coast. I loved the area but was feeling a little sad as my best friend, who was supposed to be with me, had _____ (cancel) at the last minute.

One morning, I _____ (wake) up very early and decided to collect shells on the beach. The freshness of the early morning air was _____ (delight) after being in the holiday caravan. I closed the door behind me as _____ (quiet) as I could, aware of the shapes of my parents still fast asleep in their narrow caravan bed.

It was a _____ (glory) morning. The night before, there had been a _____ (violence) storm, and I had heard huge waves _____ (crash) onto the shore. It is said that in the past many sailors sadly _____ (drown) here, their boats _____ (cruel) smashed on the rocks. By the morning, the storm had gone and the air was still and peaceful, like a patient _____ (recover) from a fever. On the horizon, a boat hooted, and above me, seagulls _____ (screech) and circled.

The tide was out and the sand was wet and firm. Eagerly, I rolled up my jeans and _____ (splash) through the cool, shallow water. Now and again a silvery fish slipped across my feet, _____ (remind) me of the underwater world that one day I would love to explore. The sand was full of shells, and I chose the most interesting-looking ones for my _____ (collect). I bent down and dug out a starfish from the sand, to _____ (inspection) its shape more closely.

The growing warmth of the sun told me that time was _____ (pass). My parents would be waking up and wondering where I was. I was reluctantly turning back when I heard a voice calling me. To my _____ (astonish), I saw my friend Caroline standing on the cliff top and waving. She later told me her family's plans had changed and they had _____ (decide) to come to the coast after all.

My brilliant holiday by the sea was now perfect!

Unit 8: The search for adventure

B Adrift on the Pacific

1 Forming questions

CB Section B1

You are interviewing a couple who survived being adrift at sea for months. Rearrange the sentences to make direct questions. Put a capital letter at the beginning and a question mark at the end.

a   you ever up hope did give

    ....

b   big how Ocean Pacific is the

    ....

c   good now you are in health

    ....

d   longer you think could survived do much how you have

    ....

e   preparations you make what journey for did the

    ....

f   is how a big whale sperm

    ....

g   your plans for future are the what

    ....

h   think were about what you while you raft on the did

    ....

i   do what taste like sharks

    ....

j   you keen are sailing still on

    ....

2 Ordering events

Put these sentences into the correct order. Write the letters on the line below.

CB Section B6

a   Before setting off on a trip now, I get my maps out and check the coastline really carefully.

b   Initially, I had quite a few problems with the boat, including nearly smashing it up on some rocks and running out of petrol miles from the shore!

c   Finally, I inspect the boat to make sure it is in good condition, and I pack my favourite food and drink for the day.

d   After that, if I am still concerned about anything, I'll ring the coastguard to ask for some advice.

e   Eventually, after saving for quite a long time, I had enough to buy a second-hand speedboat.

f   Then I use the internet to find out the times of the tides and the weather forecast.

g   Ever since my parents took me on a boating holiday as a child, I've wanted to have a boat of my own.

h   So I started to develop a much more cautious approach.

i   So as soon as I got my first job, I started saving up all my spare cash.

Order: _____

3 Reporting verbs

Choose a suitable verb from the box to complete each sentence. Do not use any verb more than once. There is one more than you need.

CB Section B10

| offered   admitted   estimated   congratulated   threatened |
| apologised   agreed   explained   complained   boasted |

a   He _____ that he was more capable than the others who had attempted to sail around the world.

b   After the disaster happened, the tour guide _____ that she had been at fault for not checking the names on the passenger list.

c   The young yachtswoman was _____ on her outstanding achievement.

d   Our neighbour has _____ to take our children to watch the boat race.

e   Ajay _____ for forgetting to send a text saying that he had arrived safely.

Unit 8: The search for adventure

f The authorities _____ that the storm damage would cost around $2 million to repair.

g We approached several companies for sponsorship, and finally a soft drinks company _____ to donate some money to the project.

h The survivors of the earthquake _____ that the ordeal had given them great inner strength.

i The ship's passengers _____ that the cabins were too small and the meals were tasteless.

4 Writing a report of an interview: Pre-listening task

CB Section B11

Draw lines to match these words to their meanings.

a peninsula   a place where nature is protected

b marine   the people who do the work on a boat

c metropolitan   a long thin strip of land surrounded by water

d reserve   relating to a large city

e crew   relating to the sea and things that live in it

Study the map, which shows a journey made by a group of people from San Diego. Write a short paragraph describing the route they took. Use linking words such as *Initially / Then / After that / Eventually / Finally*.

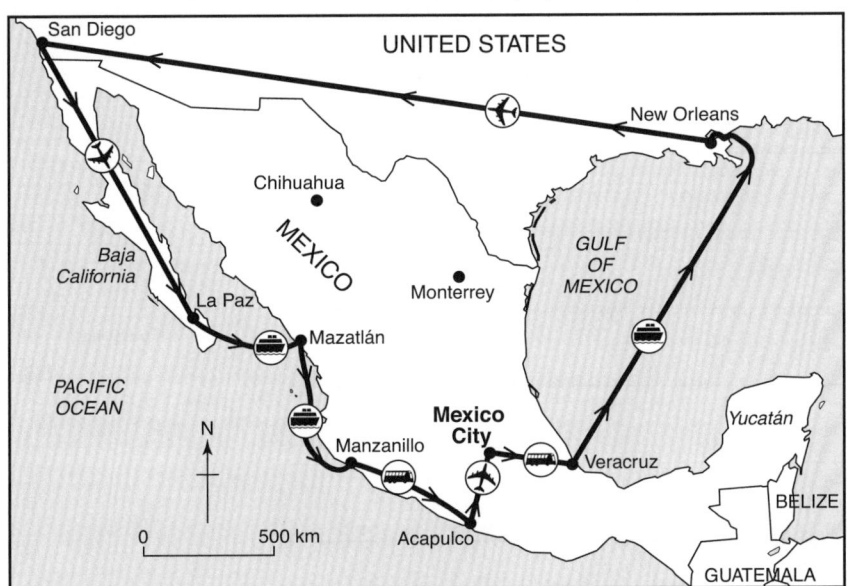

5 Writing a report of an interview: Listening task

You are going to hear an interview with Clara Sanchez, one of the young people who made the journey shown in Activity 4. Listen to the interview and make notes about the places she visited and what she did there.

La Paz: _____

Mazatlán: _____

Manzanillo: _____

Acapulco: _____

Mexico City: _____

CB Sections B4 and B11

Unit 8: The search for adventure

Veracruz: _____

New Orleans: _____

6 Writing a report of an interview: Writing task

CB Section B11

Imagine you are the journalist who interviewed Clara. Write a report for your travel magazine for young people, using the map and your notes. Make up any extra information you need or think readers will find interesting.

....
....
....
....
....
....
....
....
....
....
....
....
....

C A remarkable rescue

1 Vocabulary check

Circle or underline the correct word from each pair in *italics*.

a From the edge of the cliff, there is a *sheer / rocky* drop to the sea below.

b We were relieved to hear that Grandma had survived the operation and that her *condition / state* was stable.

c Edith came out of the exam feeling very pleased and *convicted / convinced* that she had scored high marks.

d The twins spend a lot of time playing a game in which they *chase / follow* each other and try not to get caught.

e We missed the last train home and were *stranded / shipwrecked* in Paris for the night.

f The number of casualties was *initially / primarily* reported to be over 20.

2 Language study: Defining relative clauses

> CB Section C10

Write sensible and interesting relative clauses to complete these sentences.

a On holiday I prefer to visit places where _____.

b A whale is a mammal that _____.

c 'We are hoping for a miracle,' said the man whose _____.

d A tug is small boat _____.

e That week _____ was the happiest time of my life!

f Tsunamis are unusually strong ocean waves _____.

3 Language study: Non-defining relative clauses

> CB Section C11

Correct the errors in these sentences.

a Another issue is the cost of pet insurance, that increased by 50 percent last year.

b She has two pet cats, which she really loves them.

c The zookeeper who was standing quite near the elephant, wasn't hurt when it fell.

Unit 8: The search for adventure

d There was a gift shop at the zoo, which it was very expensive.

e You'll have the chance to see the penguins being fed, which I know you'll enjoy it.

 4 Language study: Adverbs

CB Section C14

Form adverbs from the adjectives in the box to complete these sentences. Be careful with the spelling. The first one has been done as an example.

> suitable   romantic   steady   ~~extraordinary~~   extreme   simple
> immediate   dramatic   responsible

a When the ship hit an iceberg, the captain was _extraordinarily_ brave.

b We made sure our first aid box was _____ equipped with bandages, antiseptic and plasters.

c The famous actress's name has been _____ linked with the captain of a large cruise liner.

d The winds that blow _____ towards the Equator are called trade winds because cargo-carrying sailing ships used to rely on them.

e The Dead Sea is so full of salt that it is said to be _____ difficult to sink in it.

f Nathalia reacted so _____ during the crisis that she was _____ promoted to officer rank.

g The blueness of the Aegean Sea can be _____ explained by the amount of sunlight reaching the water's surface.

h The Gulf Stream is a warm ocean current that _____ affects the climate of Northern Europe.

Complete each sentence with a suitable adverb.

a I admire people who _____ ski down really steep slopes.

b Sometimes monkeys near the resort _____ attack tourists.

c The restaurant was very _____ located next to the beach so it was really easy to go there for lunch.

d Unfortunately, flying isn't a very _____ friendly way to travel.

e There's no need to speak a language totally _____ when visiting a country, but it's good to know some useful vocabulary and phrases.

f Many young people choose to travel _____ rather than going with an organised tour group.

g The tourists' minibus _____ avoided having an accident with an oncoming vehicle.

h You're not _____ thinking of doing a parachute jump, are you?

D Reacting to the unexpected

1 Analysing the narrative

Remember – a narrative should obey the simple rules of *Who? What? Where? Why? How?* and *When?* In a short story, these are often covered at the beginning so the reader can understand what is happening in the story.

CB Section D4

Read this opening to a story. Mark it ✓ if all the rules have been obeyed and ✗ if all the rules have not been followed.

> It was a golden autumn day, and Max and his father were driving towards the naval college on the coast where Max, who had recently left school, was going to start a marine technology course. Max had been so excited when his letter of acceptance had arrived, but now that they were actually setting off, he was feeling a little worried.
>
> They were not far from the college when suddenly a distressed-looking man ran into the road, waving the car to a stop. Apparently, his little boy had climbed onto the roof of their flat to rescue a kitten and was now trapped up there.

2 Ways of developing an outline

CB Section D7

Listen to Ayesha telling her friend Youssef about a memorable experience and make a list of the main points in the story.

a ....

b ....

c ....

d ....

Unit 8: The search for adventure

e ....

f ....

g ....

h ....

i ....

j ....

k ....

l ....

3 Building a story from dialogue

Use the list of events from Exercise D2 to build a story. Make up and add in extra detail to make the story more interesting. Listen to the conversation from Activity D2 again if you need to. Make sure your story has a strong opening and ending. You can write the narrative in either the first person (using 'I') or the third person (using 'she' or 'he').

CB Section D8

....

....

....

....

....

....

....

....

....

....
....
....
....
....
....

4 Text correction

Read Hugo's report for the headteacher about a Young Explorer's competition and correct the mistakes in the tenses. There are 18 mistakes to find.

> Last October, Mr Bains, our science teacher, telling us about the Young Explorer competition. He driving to school listening to the radio when he has heard an interview with an explorer. At the end of the programme, the competition was announced. To enter the competition, Mr Bains explained that we had to make a model of equipment that would be useful on an expedition. Our club getting really excited about the idea, although we were a bit nervous about it too, as it was the first time we enter a competition.
>
> We decided to make our model from toy construction bricks, which we could borrowed from younger brothers and sisters. First of all, we brainstorm our ideas and, after some disagreement, we will decide to make a sled for carrying equipment on an Arctic expedition. We wanted the sled to be original, and Finlay Hudson suggest making a sled that could also be used as a life raft. We all liked the sound of that!
>
> We experiment with different approaches, and finally we build a model that we were happy with. We have used very small bricks to make the ice axe, skis and storage boxes.
>
> We packing our model carefully and send it off. The club then forgetting about it, because we were busy with exams. To our delight, Mr Bains got an email last week saying our club win an award for the most inventive model. We were all so proud as none of us ever winning a prize before. The club will get an Explorer's Survival Kit, which included sleeping bags, ropes and a compass.
>
> Please let me know if you require further information.
>
> Hugo Yi, Year 11

5 The interrupted past continuous

One of the verbs in each of these sentences is in the wrong tense. Write the sentences out correctly on the lines.

CB Grammar spotlight

a   Everything went so well, when suddenly one of the sails on the boat tore in half.

....

b   As they set off, they both knew their car is going to break down.

....

c   The four friends drove along the dark country road when they heard a loud bang on the roof of the car.

....

d   Harriet was hit by a large wave as she was swim desperately towards the shore.

....

e   As he climbs the staircase in the old house, Oliver heard a door slowly opening behind him.

....

f   When Jim and Helen opened the door, a strange old man stood behind it.

....

> Unit 9

Animals and our world

A fresh look at zoos

1 Animal vocabulary: Parts of animals

Fill each space with a word from the box. Some words can be used more than once.

CB Section A1

| mane | feathers | paws | hooves | horns | beak | hump | scales |
| fins | claws | fur | trunk | wings | tusks |

cat camel horse bird

elephant goat fish

2 Definitions

Decide whether the following sentences are true or false. Give each one a tick (✓) or a cross (✗).

CB Section A2

a   Plants or animals that are alike in some way are a *species*.   ____

b   If an animal hunts and kills you, you have become its *prey*.   ____

c   Animals that hunt and kill live animals for food are *scavengers*.   ____

d   Animals that sleep throughout the winter are *migrating*.   ____

e   When the last animal dies, the species has become *endangered*.   ____

f   Zoo animals that give birth are *breeding in captivity*.   ____

g   Zoo animals that live in secure open spaces are in *enclosures*.   ____

Unit 9: Animals and our world

h   Animals that cannot survive outside water are *amphibians*.   _____

i   If you find a trace of a bird or animal preserved in rock, you have found a *fossil*.   _____

j   If an animal is used to living with other animals, it is *domesticated*.   _____

k   Hunting may be legal but *poaching* never is.   _____

l   If an animal is kept in a box with bars, it is in a *cage*.   _____

3 Text completion

Read this article written for a school website about the history of zoos. Fill each gap with the best word from the choices.

CB Section A4

A history of zoos

No one can be certain when zoos first began, but **(a)** _____ believe that the first 'zoo' may have belonged to Queen Hatshepsut in ancient Egypt. Ancient Chinese emperors are also thought to have collected different types of birds, fish and animals from all over their **(b)** _____. The creatures were kept in pleasant gardens where they could feel at home. Such places were essentially **(c)** _____, and the animals were kept for the pleasure and entertainment of their owners.

Although kings and queens continued to collect animals and exchange exotic creatures as gifts, it was not **(d)** _____ the 1700s that scientists began to study animals in order to **(e)** _____ them. Animals were sorted into groups and given Latin names. This meant that the same animal would have the same name wherever **(f)** _____ lived. The idea of creating a public zoo was a direct **(g)** _____ of the scientists' work. London Zoo, the first zoo to be opened to the public, was built in 1829.

Our understanding of the needs of animals in captivity has grown since the early days of public zoos. Modern zoos attempt to create natural settings **(h)** _____ their animals and to provide a reasonable amount of freedom. Wherever possible, fences, hedges and small lakes or ponds are used instead of cages to separate animals **(i)** _____ visitors. Polar bears and seals have pools to splash in. In specially darkened buildings, people can see animals which are normally only **(j)** _____ at night.

127

(k) _____, many animals find it difficult to breed in zoos. The reasons for this are not yet fully understood, **(l)** _____ it may be linked to the lack of opportunity to follow normal instincts.

a	botanists	historians	veterinarians	biologists	
b	country	area	empire	region	
c	personal	isolated	private	inclusive	
d	from	in	until	when	
e	explain	know	classify	order	
f	he	she	it	they	
g	following	result	expectation	reward	
h	in	at	for	of	
i	of	from	by	with	
j	active	alive	there	aware	
k	Despite	Although	Furthermore	Nevertheless	
l	so	but	anyway	while	

B Animal experimentation

1 Vocabulary check

Match each definition or sentence with the correct word from the box.
There are more words than there are definitions.

> virus   vitamins   vaccine   hormones   veins   blood   antibiotics
> anaesthetic   laboratory   lungs   asthma   ethical

a   A substance used to make a person immune to a disease. _____

b   Using animals to test cosmetics poses this kind of question. _____

c   These form a single organ inside your chest to enable you to breathe. _____

d   This fluid nourishes our bodies and removes waste products. _____

e	Tubes that take blood to the heart from various parts of the body.	_____
f	This medical condition causes difficulty in breathing.	_____
g	You take these to fight some kinds of infection.	_____
h	These are found in food and are needed for healthy growth.	_____
i	A tiny living particle that causes disease.	_____
j	This is the place where scientists carry out their experiments.	_____

2 Pre-listening task

Put these words and phrases into the correct definition.

> go along with   vanity   cosmetics   pharmaceutical   biased
> uninformative   see the back of   dilemma   sophisticated   lined up
> simulation   ins and outs

a If you want to _____ something, you want it to go away or disappear.

b _____ are things you put on your face or body to improve your appearance.

c A _____ is a model of a real activity.

d The _____ industry creates medicines and other health products.

e If you have something _____, it means you have it ready to use.

f If you are _____, you show an unreasonable preference based on personal opinion.

g When technology is _____, it means it's able to do many complicated things.

h   If you _____ an idea, it means you support it or agree with it.

i   The _____ of something are the detailed and complicated facts about it.

j   If something is _____, it means it doesn't give you much useful information.

k   A _____ is a problem that requires making a very difficult choice.

l   _____ is when someone is too interested in their own appearance.

3 Listening

You will hear three short recordings about animal experimentation. Read the multiple-choice questions below, then listen to the recording and circle the letter of the correct answer to complete each sentence. Listen to the recordings twice if you need to.

Recording 1

1   The girl thinks that only _____ should be used in experiments with animals.

   A cats   B monkeys   C rats

2   The boy thinks animal experimentation by _____ companies should be banned.

   A cosmetics   B pharmaceutical   C food

Recording 2

3   The scientist says that her research is used to find cures for _____.

   A heart disease B diabetes   C cancer

4   The scientist suggests that protesters outside her laboratory should _____.

   A learn more   B be removed   C stay quiet

Recording 3

5   The boy thinks animal experimentation will all be done on _____ in the future.

   A people   B bacteria   C computers

6   The girl suggests that reports on animal testing in the media are _____.

   A too common   B biased   C uninformative

4 Writing an article for the school blog

Students have been asked to contribute blog posts on the topic of animal experimentation.

CB Section B11

You decide to write a post about testing cosmetics on animals, explaining:

- why cosmetics are sometimes tested on animals
- your own opinion about this issue
- alternatives to testing cosmetics on animals and their pros and cons.

Before you start:

- decide on your angle for the blog post (Are you in favour or against? How strongly do you feel about it?)
- list the points you wish to make on a piece of paper before you start writing the post
- think about the structure and language of the post; it's probably best to follow the structure shown in the bullet points above.

Make sure your blog post:

- has a strong opening to grab your readers' attention
- uses opinion words and phrases
- uses linking words and expressions to make it easier and more interesting to read
- includes clear opinions about the issues.

5 Prepositions after verbs

CB Section B12

Complete each sentence with a suitable preposition.

a The students agreed _____ follow a set of rules during the animal experimentation debate.

b One of the students apologised _____ shouting during the debate.

c The scientist began _____ explaining what work her research project did.

d The teacher commented _____ how well some students presented their arguments.

e No one complained _____ the noise of the protesters outside.

f The report consisted _____ information about the research and recommendations for future projects.

g Although we disagreed _____ each other during the argument, we're all good friends again now.

h My best friend is still recovering _____ a serious illness.

Unit 9: Animals and our world

C Animals in sport and entertainment

1 People's opinions

CB Section C2

Match the halves to make logical sentences about hunting animals for sport. Put the correct number (1–8) in the box after each sentence beginning (a–h).

a   Rico says shooting birds is a harmless field sport, but as I see it, ☐

b   The campaigners protest against cruelty to animals but ☐

c   Although shooting is just a game to many who take part, ☐

d   Let's face it, stopping the deer hunt on Saturday ☐

e   I believe raising people's awareness is the best method of ending ☐

f   Why should people lose the pleasure of following a traditional sport ☐

g   People claim that fox hunting helps farmers keep the fox population down, yet ☐

h   What's worse: the nightmare to farmers of allowing wolves to kill their newborn lambs, ☐

1   just because some people claim it's immoral?
2   the abuse of animals in sport.
3   isn't going to be easy.
4   it is nothing but a blood sport.
5   they are perfectly happy to eat meat.
6   is it as much fun for those animals on the receiving end?
7   a ban on it would have no significant impact on the numbers in rural areas.
8   or killing these predators quickly and cleanly in a well-organised hunting event?

2 Vocabulary: Words for feelings

CB Section C4

Circle or underline the correct word from each pair in *italics*.

a   Helena was *apologetic / disgusted* by the cruel method of controlling the rabbit population.

b   The children felt *uneasy / absurd* about touching the snake, even though the owner said it was perfectly harmless.

133

c   A growing number of people feel that eating meat is *immoral / horrified* for environmental as well as humanitarian reasons.

d   They were *distressed / disrupted* to hear that the zoo would soon be closing down for good.

e   The owner of the zoo was *appealed / saddened* that so few visitors came to see the new animals.

f   Everyone agreed that Franck looked *wrong / ridiculous* in the strange animal costume.

3 Language study: Adding emphasis

Choose an adjective from the box to add emphasis to each sentence. There is one more than you need.

CB Section C5

> innocent   absurd   anxious   passionate   apologetic   magical

a   We were disturbed to hear of _____ animals being harmed for fun.

b   Some people think the idea that animals in zoos suffer more stress than those kept in laboratories is _____.

c   We were fascinated by the _____ sight of a mother bird feeding her tiny babies.

d   Desmond sent Li Huan a(n) _____ letter saying how sorry he was for forgetting their arrangement to meet.

e   By her _____ expression, we knew Leila was worried about something.

D Animals at work

1 Verb forms

Each of these sentences contains an incorrect verb form. Find and correct each one.

a   Dinosaurs have become extinct a long time ago.

b   Scientists think that early man was keeping dogs to help with hunting.

c   Lizards are feeding on small insects and plants.

Unit 9: Animals and our world

d   He needed to see a doctor because the rat had been biting his hand.

e   Ruben has sold his farm 10 years ago.

f   For many years, the camel is used for transport, especially in desert regions of the world.

g   Intensive farming methods often criticise for being harmful to the environment.

2 Vocabulary: Young animals

Which of these is *not* a young bird or animal? Circle the answer.

CB Section D6

| cub   foal   duckling   calf   cygnet   ewe   kid   lamb   kitten |

3 Vocabulary: Collective nouns

Which of these is *not* a collective noun for a group of animals, birds or fish?

CB Section D8

| herd   swarm   foal   pack   flock   shoal |

4 Vocabulary check: Farming

Circle or underline the correct word from each pair in *italics*.

a   I'm afraid the apples and pears in the *vineyard / orchard* aren't ripe enough for picking yet.

b   They keep a wide range of *hens / poultry*, including chickens, ducks and geese.

c   Local milk, butter and cheese come from the dairy *herds / flocks* kept on farms around here.

d   Do you know of any farmers who don't *grow / rear* their animals for profit?

e   Food that is produced as naturally as possible is known as *intensive / organic*.

f   Hens that live in natural conditions produce eggs described as *free range / home grown*.

g   If they don't use *pesticides / subsidies*, how will they control the insects that eat all the grain?

h   I can't see how *processed / manufactured* food can be as good for you as food that goes straight from the grower to the market.

5 Text completion

Complete this student's composition by thinking of one suitable word to fill each space.

Do the advantages of intensive farming outweigh the disadvantages?
Yes!

In the first place, who wants to go back to the olden days when food (a) _____ difficult to grow and likely to (b) _____ contaminated? People couldn't even trust the milk because (c) _____ could carry awful bacteria.

In addition, I love going into bright, clean supermarkets and choosing perfect fruit (d) _____ I know won't poison me, because all the germs (e) _____ been killed off. I don't want to go into dirty food shops (f) _____ the equipment isn't clean and (g) _____ there are unpleasant smells.

Furthermore, food these days is also (h) _____ cheaper, which means everyone can afford to eat properly. My grandparents could (i) _____ eat cheese once a week and hardly knew (j) _____ meat tasted like!

Finally, people (k) _____ that farm animals are unfairly treated but it's time we recognised what we need them for. Animals cannot talk or (l) _____ in the same way as humans. Little children enjoy pretty pictures of woolly lambs playing (m) _____ the fields, but everyone has to grow up. We need to eat and we need safe food that is cheaply produced. Why not thank intensive farming (n) _____ providing that for us?

Now do the same with this composition by another student.

Do the advantages of intensive farming outweigh the disadvantages?
No!

In the first place, we call ourselves a civilised society but our exploitation of animals (o) _____ absolutely disgusting. Farm animals are kept (p) _____ appalling and most unnatural conditions just (q) _____ that we can buy cheap meat, eggs and cheese. Intensive farming has also led (r) _____ food surpluses. Richer countries have 'butter mountains', for example, (s) _____ people in poorer countries go hungry. I think this is shocking.

CB Section D9

Unit 9: Animals and our world

In addition, the frantic demands **(t)** _____ intensive production have resulted in a disruption to the food chain. Some cattle have had a strange disease **(u)** _____ has jumped species and affected humans. Scientific interference does not stop **(v)** _____. Supermarket shelves are crammed with highly unnatural, genetically modified foods. This can only end in disaster **(w)** _____ the nation's health.

To sum up, I urge all readers to write **(x)** _____ their newspaper about animal welfare issues or post their comments online. I know some people, even if they have strong views, don't write to newspapers or post comments on social media, **(y)** _____ your views really will make a difference. It IS worth it!

List the ways in which each writer demonstrates bias towards one side of the argument and how they try to influence their readers to agree with them. Give examples where you can.

E Helping animals in danger

1 Understanding graphs

The bar chart gives information about the use of animals for cosmetics testing in a European country. Decide whether the statements are true or false, and circle your answer.

CB International overview

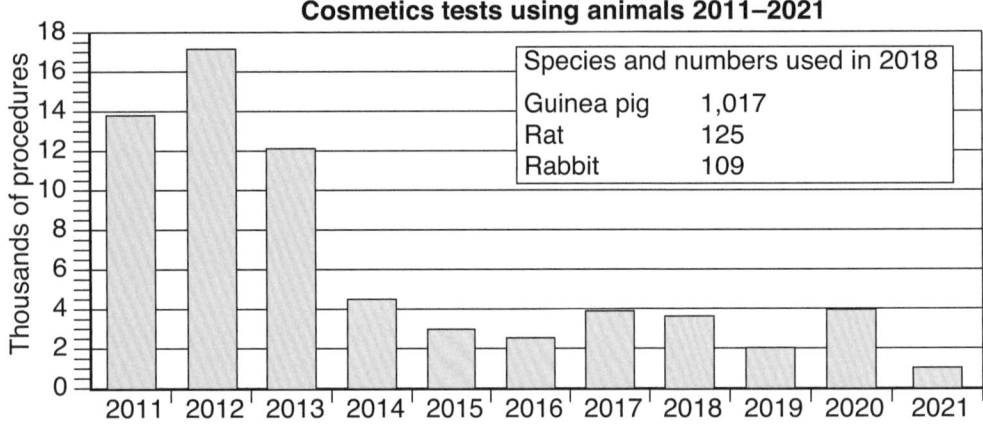

Cosmetics tests using animals 2011–2021

Species and numbers used in 2018
Guinea pig   1,017
Rat   125
Rabbit   109

a	The information covers a period of 12 years.	T / F
b	Testing peaked in 2012.	T / F
c	The sharpest fall was between 2012 and 2014.	T / F
d	Numbers rose and then fell.	T / F
e	The general trend was downwards.	T / F
f	Over a thousand different species of animals were used in the testing.	T / F

2 Proofreading a report

CB Section E4

Li's class has recently visited an animal sanctuary, and the headteacher has asked her to write a report about the visit. In the report, there is one extra word in each sentence. Correct Li's report by deleting the extra words. The first sentence has been done for you.

> Our class visit to the animal sanctuary to see ~~with~~ the giant panda and the newborn twin giant panda cubs was so thrilling. We were all looking very forward to it so much. All of us felt we knew so a lot about the cubs before the visit. In our biology lesson, we had learnt that they had were sleeping in warm cots called incubators and special techniques were needed to care for them.
>
> Mrs Lun had been told us about the way in which, in the wild, a mother who has twins may struggle to feed both babies and may abandon one of them. In the zoo, however, staff take one cub to the incubator while the mother her feeds the other one.

It was amazing for to see this happen in real life. The zoo staff they used a stick of sugar cane to distract the mother while a member of staff took one of the cubs away.

We all wanted to take photographs, and everyone was able to get there fantastic pictures of the cubs. We also saw how the cubs trying to move by pushing their legs backwards. We were told they only weighed about 113 grams when they been were born, which is about the same as our phones. We don't know their names yet, because the cubs will not be named until they are 100 days of old.

On the way back to school, we decided to upload on the photos onto the school website. Mrs Lun suggested we also write a fun online quiz based on the notes from the staff gave us.

We all appreciated the experience so much, and we are going to treasure it the memories for the rest of our lives.

3 Improving a report

Match these extracts from students' writing with extracts 1–8 written in a more complex and less repetitive style.

a It is wrong to kill wild animals to make medicines. These medicines do not make you get better from illnesses even when they take them.

b This means children who are not born at the moment can't see them to know what they were like when they are born because they won't be there to see them.

c The people who work in the zoo tried to get them to have babies but they didn't want to have babies in the zoo, but they would have them if they were back in their homes.

d These big animals were in these kind of like cage things, and I saw that these great big animals were not happy that they were in them.

e If you give some money now, it's going to help and you don't need to give a lot to save them because all the money you give we are going to send to them.

f Blood sport is not really like that bad a sport like everyone says, and we should worry instead about helping children who haven't got enough money for the hospital.

g Some people get pets as gifts and then they don't want them so they just throw them away, and this place has people who find them in the street and they are so good to these poor little animals.

h I didn't like what he did, and it made me feel so bad when I thought about it that I never wanted to think about it again.

CB Section E5

1 Some animals dislike breeding in captivity.
2 Why should animals be killed for useless medical research?
3 Why all the fuss about bullfighting when children are suffering terribly through lack of basic medical care?
4 I was sickened by his appalling behaviour.
5 The rescue workers at the centre for injured and abandoned animals are really tender towards them.
6 It's horrifying to think that future generations may never know these magnificent creatures.
7 Donating even a few pounds makes a significant difference to the charity's life-saving efforts.
8 Can we even guess at the suffering of a huge beast trapped in a tiny space?

4 The past perfect passive

CB Grammar spotlight

The most common mistake students make using the past perfect passive is to use the past simple passive instead:

The next day, I found out that the male tiger was moved to another zoo. ✗

The next day, I found out that the male tiger had been moved to another zoo. ✓

Also, remember to use the past perfect in the if clause of third conditional sentences, <u>not</u> would + have + been + past participle:

It would have been easier if guns would not have been invented. ✗

It would have been easier if guns had not been invented. ✓

Use the prompts to create sentences containing the past perfect passive.

a when / I / next went / zoo / many new trees / planted in / animals' enclosures

   ....

b we / eat / fresh fish / dinner / catch / by locals / nearby lake

   ....

c if / the rabbit / catch / Martha / would / be / very upset

   ....

d Tiffany / notice / new make-up / not / test / on animals

   ....

e what / you / do / if / the zoo / force / to close / ?

   ....

Unit 10
The world of work

A The rewards of work

1 Skills and qualities for work

Complete each definition with the correct word from the box.

CB Section A2

> company director   novelist   nursery teacher   miner   cellist
> journalist   plumber   labourer   dentist   carpenter   midwife
> interpreter   firefighter   interior designer   chauffeur
> choreographer

a A(n) _____ takes care of your teeth.

b A(n) _____ writes fiction books.

c A(n) _____ translates one language into another.

d A(n) _____ designs the insides of houses.

e A(n) _____ puts out fires.

f A(n) _____ writes for a newspaper.

g A(n) _____ plays a musical instrument.

h A(n) _____ manages a large and successful business.

i A(n) _____ works with very young children.

j A(n) _____ does physical work in building, repairing roads, etc.

k A(n) _____ makes things out of wood.

l A(n) _____ extracts coal or metals from under the ground.

m A(n) _____ is employed to drive a car for a rich or important person.

n A(n) _____ delivers babies.

o A(n) _____ repairs water pipes.

p A(n) _____ creates dances for the stage.

Now think of three more occupations and write their definitions.

....

....

....

2 More work-related vocabulary

Choose the correct word from the box to complete each sentence. Use each word only once. Not all words can be used.

CB Section A9

> launch   investing   profitable   brand   research   packaging
> campaign   manufacturing   competitive   consumers

a   They carried out further market _____ to assess the likely success of the idea.

b   It's difficult to make money in her business because it's a very _____ market.

c   They want to increase production and are _____ in a new factory.

d   The company had to close down because it wasn't _____.

e   We plan to _____ our new range of swimwear in April.

f   The directors met to plan their advertising _____ for the following year.

g   Have you tried this new _____ of coffee? It's really delicious.

h   The cosmetics company gave up the idea of _____ a new kind of lipstick.

Unit 10: The world of work

3 Idioms

Draw lines to match the work-related idioms to their meanings.

CB Section A10

a line of work — to have all the latest information about something so you can do it well

b get your foot in the door — to be in charge and make important decisions

c call the shots — to watch someone very closely and check what they're doing

d be in the red — the kind of job that you do

e get up to speed — to have less than zero in the bank

f breathe down someone's neck — to enter a company at a low level with the hope of being more successful in the future

Now use the idioms to complete the sentences below. You may need to change the form of some of the idioms.

a It took Magda a few days to _____ after starting her new job.

b Even though he only got an administrative assistant position, Sergei was happy he had _____ at such a well-respected company.

c Leila was worried because her business had _____ for three successive months.

d Asking what _____ you're in is a common question at parties and social events.

e I hate it when my boss is _____ all day at work! It's a relief when he's out of the office.

f The Managing Director told Mikhail that he was _____ at work while she was away at the trade fair.

4 Understanding visual data

CB Section A13

Study the bar charts on the next page, then circle whether the following information is true or false. Note the correct information for any that are false.

a The most popular choice for female students in 2017 was hotel and catering, whereas for male students it was marketing.   T / F

....

143

b There was a dramatic rise between 2017 and 2021 in the number of female students studying engineering. T / F

....

c The least popular course overall in 2021 was hairdressing. T / F

....

d The number of female students studying marketing almost doubled between 2017 and 2021. T / F

....

e More female students than male students chose the business course in 2021. T / F

....

f Business grew in popularity with both male and female students between the two years. T / F

....

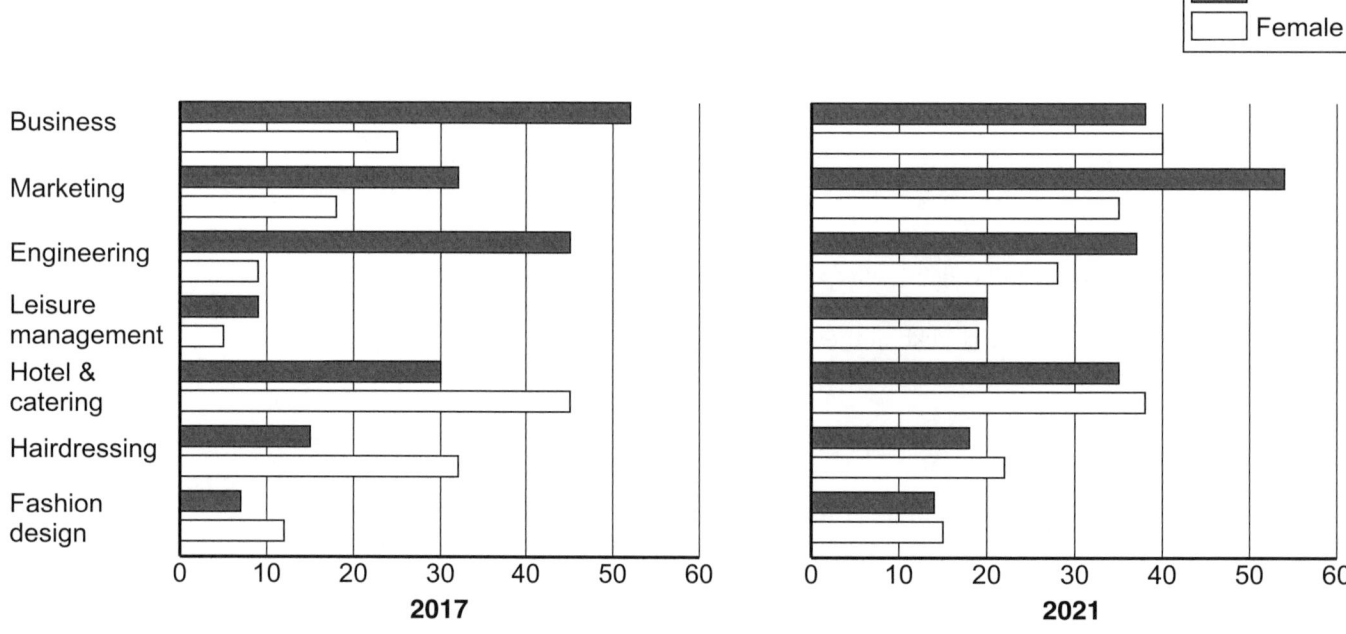

City Vocational College: first-year students

Unit 10: The world of work

B Facts and figures

1 Approximations

Do these approximations make logical sense? Give each sentence either a tick (✓) or a cross (✗).

CB Section B1

a   The company was worried when the majority of people interviewed, almost 20 percent, could not remember seeing its adverts on TV. _____

b   Very few students, about four out of five in the survey, expect to get a job immediately after graduating. _____

c   About 5 percent of students, that's one in 20, say the long-term prospects are more important when choosing their career than the starting salary. _____

d   Nearly a third (63 percent) were satisfied with the careers counselling they had received. _____

e   Getting on for half (49 percent) of respondents gave location near to home as a reason for choosing their present employment. _____

f   We were very surprised when we read that nearly a quarter of local residents (14 percent) had complained about teenagers making a noise at night. _____

2 Questioning and criticising statistics

Write the correct number (1–8) in the box to match the halves to make complete sentences. There is one extra 'second half'.

CB Sections B2 and B3

a   The government investigation pleased everyone, as it finally exposed the facts about ☐

b   We were angry when the politicians said that teenagers are happy to be out of work because ☐

c   Local people feel annoyed about the closure of the clinic, and a public meeting has been called so that they can ☐

d   We were furious when we read the article claiming that young people are to blame for the problems in the community. It's a total ☐

e   The bus company's report is distorting the truth when it claims a high level of satisfaction with the bus service. Everyone ☐

f   It's ridiculous to say that no limit should be set on working hours. Who on earth ☐

g   The report, which claims that doctors in poorer districts are not as good as those who work in affluent areas, is misleading because it is ☐

1. explain why they are upset.
2. distortion of the truth.
3. how much water contamination there had been in the town.
4. it hides the real truth about lack of jobs.
5. I know thinks it's terrible.
6. dreamt that idea up?
7. didn't provide the truth about the results.
8. not comparing like with like.

3 Rewriting in a more formal style

Rewrite this report in a more formal style.

Remember that you need to avoid:

- slang
- colloquialisms
- contractions
- rhetorical questions, question forms and question tags.

CB Section B5

> Have you ever done work experience? Well, I did some recently at a roller-skate and skateboard shop, and it was well good. The thing I was asked to do was to speak to customers when they came in to try and get them to buy our stuff. I mean, I've been skateboarding for ages, so what I don't know about skateboarding isn't worth knowing, if you know what I mean . . . The boss there was cool and we got on like a house on fire. She said I was the best work experience student she'd had, like forever! That really made my day. Anyway, I learnt loads of stuff, like using the till, trying to get shoppers to buy more, so not just a skateboard but the elbow and knee protectors too and maybe even a helmet, know what I mean. I wouldn't mind working there weekends, you know, for proper money not just work experience. Rating: a big 9 out of 10 from me!

Unit 10: The world of work

....
....
....
....
....
....
....
....
....

C Internet marketing

1 Vocabulary check

Choose the correct word from the box to complete each sentence. There is one more word than you need.

CB Section C3

| engagement   credibility   followers   niche market   target |
| audience   endorsement   promoted |

a   The company was targeting a _____ with their new cookbook aimed at working single parents.

b   The huge number of likes for the promotional video suggested a high level of _____ with the intended market.

c   After only six months in the job, Lu's enthusiasm and ability led her to be _____ to store manager.

d   The company's _____ was questioned after the advertising campaign proved to be a complete disaster.

e   The organisation decided to use social media to reach its _____ of teenagers and those in their twenties.

f   The celebrity they've chosen for their marketing drive has well over four million _____ on a range of social-media platforms.

2 Common work-related expressions

CB Section C7

Decide whether these sentences make logical sense. Give each one a tick (✓) or a cross (✗). Think carefully about the meanings of the expressions in *italics*.

a   You take a lot of rest if you work *around the clock*. _____

b   You're ignoring a problem when you *turn a blind eye* to it. _____

c   Being the office *dogsbody* is rewarding, well-paid work. _____

d   Most people are dissatisfied if they're *stuck at home* all day. _____

e   *Top-of-the-range* brands of coffee are usually the least expensive. _____

f   There are too many people giving you orders if you are *your own boss*. _____

g   When people disagree, they are *not seeing eye-to-eye*. _____

h   People who are *high-flyers* usually work in the airline industry. _____

i   If you are *out of work*, you are unemployed. _____

Guess the meaning of the words and phrases in *italics* from their context.

a   Sales continued to fall until the company *went bust*.

    ....

b   The farmer decided to *diversify*, so as well as keeping cattle, he offers holiday accommodation to tourists.

    ....

c   The factory sells directly to the consumer and, by cutting out the *middleman*, they keep prices down.

    ....

d It was difficult to run the business on his own, so he went *into partnership*.

D Recruitment with a difference

1 Vocabulary check

CB Section D2

Choose the best option from the choices in *italics* to complete the sentences. Think carefully about the meaning of the words and expressions in bold before you answer.

a Stephane took a **crash course** in Arabic sign language that lasted for *just four weeks / about a year / over three years*.

b Simon is very **tactful** and often *hurts people's feelings / hugs his friends / chooses his words carefully*.

c Louisa wanted to look **presentable** for the interview, so she *prepared some questions to ask / bought a new suit / thought carefully about what she might be asked*.

d **Sign language** is one way of helping to break down the language *barrier / disorder / learning*.

e I was **spoilt** as a child because my parents *were very strict with me / bought me anything I wanted / separated when I was young*.

f On my work experience, I had a **mentor** who *was also learning what to do / helped me find a suitable company / showed me exactly what to do*.

2 Reading for gist

CB Section D3

Add the capitalisation, punctuation and paragraphing to this text. There are three paragraphs.

jan benson is employed as a human resources assistant for a big clothing chain in Scotland the main part of her role is recruiting new staff to work at the company HR work is often stereotyped as lacking in excitement says jan but it can offer a fulfilling career to anyone who has a genuine desire to make organisations more efficient jan took a degree in economics at birmingham university before deciding she was interested in working in human resources I started as an assistant to an HR officer last august and have been studying for my qualifications in HR management in the evenings explains jan its hard work but worth it as im able to go on earning while im gaining qualifications the aspect jan most enjoys about her work is the challenge of gaining the respect of the store managers im learning from my boss mrs shah that its essential to try to understand the managers needs in terms of the kind of staff they're looking for rather than just imposing my views on them she explains

Read your punctuated text and circle the letter of the best option to complete these sentences.

1   In paragraph 1, we learn that

    A   Jan disagrees with many people's opinion of HR.

    B   Jan wished she worked for a larger organisation.

    C   Jan feels she's already made her company more efficient.

2   In paragraph 2, we learn that

    A   Jan chose her degree course based on her career aims.

    B   Jan is both working and doing a course to aid her career.

    C   Jan is pleased she has already gained some qualifications.

3   In paragraph 3, we learn that

    A   Jan finds it difficult to give advice to store managers.

    B   Jan feels her supervisor provides her with good advice.

    C   Jan loves helping managers by giving advice to new staff.

Unit 10: The world of work

3 Language study: Similes

CB Section D7

Circle or underline the most suitable word from each pair in *italics* to complete each simile.

a   Wow, it's like an *icebox / oven* in here – can I open the window and let some cool air in?

b   My boss told me off for being late – I felt like a naughty *little child / big bad wolf* again.

c   The marketing team work together like a *fast sports car / well-oiled machine*.

d   My colleague just doesn't listen – it's like talking to a *woolly hat / brick wall*.

e   I was really nervous at the interview – I was shaking like a *tree / leaf*.

f   He was so pleased to have been offered the job – it was as if he'd *had a good dream / won a million dollars*.

4 Phrasal verbs

CB Section D9

Complete each sentence with a phrasal verb from the box. Do not use any verb more than once.

| drew up | let down | turned down | put him down | drew out |
| turned up |

a   Anna's application was _____ as she was too young for the training scheme.

b   When none of his friends offered to help him, Benito felt very _____.

c   We _____ a list of all the things we wanted to achieve in our new business.

d   Ali was younger and smaller than everyone else in the group but no one ever _____.

e   The manager's skilful leadership _____ the best qualities in her staff.

f   Leah finally _____ when her friend had been waiting over half an hour.

151

E Preparing for work

1 Reading, analysis and writing

Read the text and underline the most suitable word from each pair in *italics*.

CB Section E3

When you are choosing a future career, good careers advice **(a)** *are / is* essential. An expert careers adviser is trained both to **(b)** *give / share* you information and to assess your suitability for careers that appeal **(c)** *with / to* you.

Being friendly, responsible, honest and punctual **(d)** *are / were* useful qualities in most careers. Achievements at school in sport, being a prefect, helping to organise school trips, or experience outside school **(e)** *such / like* as doing voluntary work in the community, will be regarded positively by the careers adviser. It will also provide them with valuable **(f)** *concerns / information* about your interests and personal qualities. They will also want to know your predicted exam grades, **(g)** *if / as* your results are not yet known.

When offering information about a particular career, the careers adviser will want to **(h)** *answer / know* your level of knowledge of that career. For example, many students say they want a job in 'engineering'. Engineering is **(i)** *in / a* broad field, covering a wide range of different occupations, so you will be helped to narrow down the choice and come **(j)** *to / in* a better understanding of specific kinds of work. A careers adviser can also be useful when you **(k)** *has / have* decided you want a job, say, outdoors, but again have little idea **(l)** *of / around* the type of work you could do. They will **(m)** *guide / help* you explore the options and consider related careers, from agriculture **(n)** *to / with* leisure management.

Career progression is a further important aspect that the careers adviser will be able to explain, so that you can consider the type of position you **(o)** *might / would* hold **(p)** *from / in* 10 years' time and what you might have to do to get there.

If you visit a college to enquire about courses **(q)** *which / what* interest you, be prepared to ask some questions of your own. Finding out **(r)** *which / how* many graduates of a course **(s)** *found / suggested* employment in their field after qualifying is particularly important.

Other ways of gaining insight into the world of work **(t)** *include / of* . . .

Unit 10: The world of work

....
....
....
....
....

Answer these questions about the text.

1   What is the purpose of this text?

    ....

2   Which of the following best summarises the second paragraph?

    A   suggestions of what to ask your careers adviser about

    B   how you should behave when you meet the careers adviser

    C   things that your careers adviser should know about you

3   Which of the following best summarises the third paragraph?

    A   things to think about before seeing the careers adviser

    B   how your careers adviser will be able to help you

    C   the range of jobs careers advisers know about

Complete the sentence at the end of the final paragraph, then write two additional sentences to complete the text on the lines above.

2 Correcting a report for the headteacher

CB Section E10

Students in Fatima's Year 11 class did a week's work experience with an engineering company. The headteacher has asked Fatima to write a report, giving her views on the experience. Add the punctuation to Fatima's report and then decide where the paragraphs should go.

> we all really appreciated our work experience at Le Yung Motorcycles at first, students did not want to do work experience because we had a stereotyped idea of what working in a factory was like we thought the factory was going to be noisy and dirty and we would be longing for the day to end in fact, we found out that in a modern factory like Le Yung Motorcycles, nothing could be further from the truth the factory itself was clean and pleasant, and the machines were quiet after being shown around the factory, to our surprise, we were told we could operate some of

> the machines ourselves we felt proud as we walked through the door marked 'Staff Only' and were given our special work uniforms i personally loved working with the supervisor, Mr Zu, who operated a large machine used to repair damaged engines, and I know other students had similar good experiences everyone in the company encouraged us to think of engineering as a career with many possibilities since doing work experience, I have become interested in doing an engineering degree and others in the group are thinking of jobs in marketing, design or sales for an engineering company.

3 Pre-listening task

Draw lines to match the words and phrases to their meanings.

CB Section E13

a   taken aback   despite what has been said or what you might think

b   nonetheless   like a person when you first meet them

c   laid-back   very surprised

d   take to someone   learn something new

e   hot under the collar   relaxed and calm

f   pick something up   angry about something

4 Listening

Listen to three young people talking about their first job. Match the ideas below with each of the speakers. You can use each speaker more than once.

CB Section E13

Which speaker:

a   was surprised how kind his boss was? ☐

b   soon felt extremely tired by the work? ☐

c   didn't realise how much they were learning? ☐

d   had a problem with one of their colleagues? ☐

e   could use skills they had learnt at school? ☐

f   liked the relaxed atmosphere at their workplace? ☐

Unit 10: The world of work

Now listen to the recording again and choose the best option to complete these sentences.

1 Speaker 1's role in the architect's office:

   A has become more challenging the longer she has been there.

   B still mainly includes boring and repetitive tasks.

   C is similar to that of much more experienced colleagues.

2 Speaker 2 felt that learning new things:

   A was easy due to getting lots of advice.

   B made him much more talkative.

   C stopped him from getting tired.

3 Speaker 3's experience of working in a garage:

   A was challenging due to having difficult customers.

   B was very different to how she imagined it.

   C was not a positive move for her career.

5 Superlatives

CB Grammar spotlight

Complete each sentence with the superlative form of the adjective in brackets.

a   His elegant appearance and knowledge of other languages made Laurence seem like _____ man she had ever met. (*sophisticated*)

b   This is _____ winter we have had in living memory. (*bad*)

c   Anya is _____ girl in the class and always gets top marks. (*clever*)

d   She works for one of _____ companies in the country. (*successful*)

e   Mr Benita thought Joanna was _____ person he had ever worked with. (*lazy*)

f   Everyone in the team made valid suggestions, but Max's ideas were _____. (*good*)

6 Adverbs of degree

Correct the mistakes with adverbs of degree in these sentences. One sentence has no mistakes.

a His work wasn't perfect but it was enough good.

....

b Marta's new sales targets were very not realistic nor achievable.

....

c They had a lovely picnic but didn't go swimming as the water was too cold.

....

d The meal was delicious but the restaurant was little noisy.

....

e She expected the new assistant to be bad-tempered rather but, in fact, he was extremely charming.

....

f All of the countries in the region have a bit different cultures.

....

CB Grammar spotlight

> Acknowledgements

The authors and publishers acknowledge the following sources of copyright material and are grateful for the permissions granted. While every effort has been made, it has not always been possible to identify the sources of all the material used, or to trace all copyright holders. If any omissions are brought to our notice, we will be happy to include the appropriate acknowledgements on reprinting.

Thanks to the following for permission to reproduce images:

Cover Andriy Onufriyenko/GI; *Inside* **Unit 1:** Bettmann/GI; Marco Geber/GI; Yinyang/GI; Bettmann/GI; Ridofranz/GI; **Unit 2:** Tuaindeed/GI; Dusanpetkovic/GI; Morsa Images/GI; Santje09/GI; **Unit 3:** Ingmar Kamalagharan/GI; Antagain/GI; Gawrav Sinha/GI; Santiago Urquijo/GI; Andrew Merry/GI; **Unit 4:** Prisma By Dukas/GI; Kateryna Kovarzh/GI; David Malan/GI; Jimmyjamesbond/GI; **Unit 5:** Lew Robertson/GI; Oliver Helbig/GI; Kali9/GI; **Unit 6:** Peter Dazeley/GI; Johner Images/GI; Lordrunar/GI; **Unit 7:** Donnichols/GI; Eli_Asenova/GI x2; Jasmin Merdan/GI; Peter Dazeley/GI; **Unit 8:** Geraint Rowland Photography/GI; Ivan/GI; James Warwick/GI; **Unit 9:** Clinton Weaver/GI; Morsa Images/GI; **Unit 10:** sturti/GI; Jupiter Images/GI

GI = Getty Images